Affirmations®
PUBLISHING HOUSE
living words

First published in 2012
Copyright © Affirmations Publishing House 2012

Published by
Affirmations Publishing House
34 Hyde Street, Bellingen NSW 2454 Australia
t: +61 2 6655 2350
e: sales@affirmations.com.au
www.affirmations.com.au

Designed by Jo Kuipers Design
Edited by Karen Ransome and Michelle Merrifield

Images © Gary Howard, Alana In Love, Corne Lategen, shutterstock.com, istockphoto.com.

ISBN 978-0-9808150-9-2

10 9 8 7 6 5 4 3 2

While every effort has been made to acknowledge the author of the quotations used,
please notify the publisher if this has not occurred.

Designed in Australia, printed in China on recycled paper using vegetable based inks.

breathe
bend
BLOSSOM

Michelle Merrifield

aum shanti

Steeped in gratitude, I would like to dedicate this book to my gurus, my gurus' gurus, my family, friends and fellow yogis who have inspired me on my journey thus far.

A special thanks goes to Karen Ransome. Without her guidance, love and support, this book would not be here.

contents

about michelle merrifield

Michelle Merrifield holds internationally recognised qualifications in yoga and pilates, having studied extensively in New York, India, Bali and Australia.

As owner and operator of the Essence of Living studio at Mermaid Beach on Queensland's Gold Coast, she has built a loyal and regular following of more than 5000 students, as well as providing in-house yoga and pilates programs to major corporations, charities, schools and community groups.

In 2008, Michelle established the Essence of Living International Academy. As a registered training organisation, the Academy's teacher training courses attract students from all over Australia and as far afield as the UK, USA, Canada, Brazil, Norway and Germany.

Michelle also hosts regular yoga retreats in Bali and Byron Bay, and has recently launched a series of yoga and pilates DVDs.

On a personal level, Michelle embraces a strong spiritual activism approach to yoga as a lifestyle, following the Jivamukti Yoga method founded by Sharon Gannon and David Life.

my story

My mother took me to my first yoga class when I was just 16 years of age. The classes were being held at our local surf club on the Gold Coast and I was pretty sure I'd fit right in.

I'd been a competitive athlete all through my school years. Surfing was definitely my strong suit but I was normally pretty good at most sports. I was strong. I was fit. I was used to training hard and pushing myself to the limit. Yoga was going to be a breeze.

How wrong I was!

Unlike my mother and sister and all my friends, I couldn't touch my toes or do a backbend or get my head anywhere near my knees in a forward fold. I couldn't even manage a cross-legged sitting pose. I had absolutely no flexibility whatsoever.

Aside from the humiliation of being one of the worst in the class – by a long margin! - the one thing I did get out of that first yoga session was that incredible feeling of elation as the energy hummed through my body bringing every cell to life.

I was hooked.

And there was no way my body's lack of flexibility was going to get the better of me. I kept going back and at every class, I pushed and strained, trying to force my joints to bend and twist and stretch further into all those pretzel-like positions.

But the more I tried – the more I wanted it – the further away it seemed to be.

With little progress being made, I decided to focus on pilates, earning my Mat Pilates teaching qualifications while I studied a Business degree at university.

My fairy godmother – Cheryl-Anne Leary – magically appeared in 2004. A well-known yoga teacher, she invited me to be her partner in establishing Essence of Living – a small yoga and pilates studio in my home suburb of Mermaid Beach.

Whilst we were blessed to find a team of wonderful yoga instructors to take the various classes, they had an alarmingly regular tendency to head off to India, Nepal or Tibet on soul-searching expeditions. Even more alarmingly, I was forced to teach yoga classes in their absence.

To say that I didn't feel I was good enough would be the understatement of the year! Despite the fact that I'd been practicing yoga for several years by that stage, most of the students were far more advanced than me.

For the sake of the business I needed to gain qualifications in order to be able to teach.

Studying in the mystical mountain village of Ubud, I met my first beloved guruji Emil Wendel. Emil has been living in Asia since the mid-seventies, studying Indian and Chinese philosophy. For me, he transformed the physical practice of yoga into a way of life.

From Emil I learnt that on the mat, as in life, yoga is about being patient and compassionate – towards others and towards yourself. It's about letting go and accepting what the universe presents you with and having faith that all is unfolding as it should be.

From a physical standpoint, the moment I stopped trying to force myself into those twists and backbends, the moment I softened up and let go, my body instantly opened up and began to unfold naturally.

From a spiritual standpoint, the most important realisation was that there was so much more to learn.

The following year, I travelled to India to study under Emil once again at the Brahmini Yoga School's intensive teacher training program where I learnt even more about the practice … and myself.

I came across my next teachers in the pages of a book – Jivamukti Yoga: Practices for Liberating Body and Soul by Sharon Gannon and David Life. One of the nine recognised styles of hatha yoga practised worldwide today, Sharon and David created the Jivamukti Yoga method in 1984; integrating the physical asana-based practice with a commitment to ahimsa (non-violence) in relation to animals and the environment.

Described as "a path to enlightenment through compassion for all beings", their teaching revolves around animal rights, veganism, environmentalism and social activism because, as Sharon says, "what could be more physical than what you eat, where you live and who you live with?"

I read their book from front to back in one sitting. Their words resonated in every fibre of my being. I needed to learn more.

It meant emptying my bank account and travelling to the Jivamukti Yoga School in New York where I encountered some of my most life-changing experiences to date.

First and foremost, the calibre of students was incredible. Not just physically, but spiritually. The word 'jivamukti' translates as 'liberation while living' and the people I met studying the month-long teacher training course truly embraced the 'liberation' of 'living' yoga in their everyday life.

They were strong animal activists, vegans, environmentalists – all the tenets I had believed in for so many years. I had found my spiritual home.

However even more significantly, at the Jivamukti Yoga Centre, I met Alanna Kaivalya. In addition to teaching yoga classes at the centre, this fabulously talented woman is a singer/songwriter and author who brings her love of music into the yoga practice.

Taking me under her expansive wings, Alanna mentored me and shared her teachings. She is, without doubt, one of the most instrumental gurus I have had the pleasure to work with.

On my second trip to New York to undertake my apprenticeship, Alanna introduced me to the object of love itself – Sri Dharma Mittra.

A small, humble Brazilian master with a cheeky smile, Sri Dharma has devoted more than 50 years of his life to the study, practice and teaching of yoga as the pathway to radiant health and spiritual development. He works tirelessly to promote ahisma through veganism, (yoga diet) and kindness to all living beings, and every student who comes to his class is embraced "as part of my family".

Known for his humility, humour, joy and kindness, he is revered as 'the Rock of Yoga' and 'the teacher's teacher'.

Drawing on the spiritual inspiration of all these incredible teachers, I have been truly blessed to be able to combine my own personal philosophy, interests and lifestyle into a successful career.

The Essence of Living Yoga and Pilates Studio continues to go from strength to strength, with over 5000 students on the books at last count. A team of fantastic teachers has allowed me to expand beyond the studio to corporate workplaces, schools, retirement homes and even into local parks and community centres where we share the benefits of yoga and pilates through the Gold Coast City Council's extensive Active and Healthy lifestyle program.

In 2008, the Essence of Living International Academy was launched, providing accredited teacher training programs for yoga and pilates instructors who travel from all over the world to attend our courses.

Through all of my teaching, I am still committed to continuing my own studies. For four months of the year, I wake up at 4am for the one-hour drive to Byron Bay where I have found a small Ashtanga yoga shala run by Dena Kingsberg – a strong, dynamic inspirational woman whose certification comes from the great founder of the Ashtanga Yoga Research Institute, Sri Pattabhi Jois.

I always say that, as a teacher, I am merely the messenger, passing along what I have learnt from all the incredible gurus I have been blessed to work with.

'Breathe, Bend, Blossom' is my humble interpretation of what they have taught me over many years and how I have come to apply the lessons of yoga in my own life:

That it starts with the breath – the lifeforce – the union between our individual spirits and the divine universal energy;

That our body is the temple that houses the spirit so we bend and stretch and twist and fold to keep that temple healthy and strong;

It is only when we have tended to the body, mind and soul that we can truly blossom and use the lessons of yoga to make the wold a more beautiful and peaceful place.

What I know for sure is that the practice of yoga has organically shifted my energy and realigned me to my higher self. It has given me clear insight into my life's purpose and has set me on the right pathway to achieve it.

I also know for sure that it can do the same for you.

surfing prana

Growing up in the seaside suburb of Mermaid Beach, I was blessed to be woken each day by the sound of the ocean. I'd fly out of bed, grab my surfboard and head down to the shore to dive into Mama Ocean's pearly blue swells.

As a teenager, I joined the competitive circuit; travelling the globe to Indonesia, South America, Central America, Hawaii, Fiji and more, in search of the perfect wave.

Whilst I spend my time these days surfing prana on my yoga mat, I still hit the waves whenever my busy schedule allows.

Yoga and surfing, I've discovered, have much in common.

Sitting out on my board, balanced between water and sky, I experience a deep sense of oneness with the universe.

I am alone with my thoughts, totally removed from the distractions of everyday life. I breathe. Slowly. Deeply. Savouring the sweet pure flavour of the ocean air.

As the wave builds and gathers beneath me, my body bends to the challenge of riding the swell of energy towards the shore. It takes strength. Balance. Crystal clear focus.

And, if I'm lucky, the universe blossoms; sending a dolphin, albatross, manta ray or whale to share this moment of divine grace.

I am alone with my thoughts, totally removed from the distractions of everyday life.

I breathe. Slowly. Deeply. Savouring the sweet pure flavour of the ocean air.

The first thing we do when we are born is inhale.

In between is life.

The last thing we do when we die is exhale.

breathe

breathe
In the beginning, the middle and
the end, there is always the breath,
our inner lifeforce and our connection
with the universal energy flow

breathe

Like a finely tuned woodwind instrument, our bodies need oxygen in order to sing and play. The sweeter the quality of the breath, the sweeter the quality of the harmony in our lives.

Whether you practice yoga as a physical exercise or embrace it as an all-encompassing life philosophy, the breath is at the heart of everything. The beginning. The middle. The end. And whatever comes after that.

Many spiritualists believe that the breath is what connects us to the energy of the universe.

It's not hard to follow their logic: In nature, the trees so deeply rooted in the earth absorb carbon dioxide and convert it into the oxygen that we inhale with every breath. We, in turn, exhale carbon dioxide which the trees need to keep them – and ultimately, us – alive.

It is one long, continuous, connected cycle between humans, nature, the earth and everything else in the universe.

Is that a little bit too 'far out' for you? How about looking at it on a more personal level.

Most of us breath shallowly … aimlessly … without conscious thought. When we are stressed or angry or frightened, we breathe faster. When we are calm and relaxed and at peace, we breathe more slowly.

Through conscious breathing, we can easily turn this equation around: By controlling the pace of our breath, we can control our mind and emotions.

If your desire is to live your life in a state of peace and serenity, take control of your breath and inhale slowly … deeply … with deliberate, conscious thought.

Still a little too esoteric, you say? Well let's bring it back to pure biology: The human body can survive up to four weeks without food and somewhere between eight and fourteen days without water. Without oxygen, death comes within a matter of minutes.

Whichever way you want to look at it, the breath is our most precious commodity. Through the practice of complete yogic breathing, we can prolong our life, improve the quality of our life and forge a connection with the eternal lifeforce of the universe.

slow it down

In India, they say we only have a certain number of breaths in our lives. The faster we breathe, the faster we will use up the breaths we have been given.

The average respiratory rate for an adult is around twelve breaths per minute.

Imagine if we could reduce that down to six slow, deep conscious breaths.

According to those Indian sages, we would be adding years to our life … and life to our years.

We only have to look at the animal kingdom for proof: Rodents are among the fastest-breathing creatures on earth and have the shortest lifespan. A tortoise takes around four to five breaths per minute and will generally live up to 200 years or more.

Notice, too, all the negative emotions associated with faster breathing: stress, anger, fear, uncertainty, panic. Surely our ultimate goal must be to live our lives in peace, harmony, serenity, confidence and all the other positive emotions associated with slow, deep, relaxed breathing.

The amazing thing about facing the world with your head held high and an open heart is that you will slowly begin to feel more positive, more confident and lighter in spirit.

posture perfect

The quality of your breath is directly related to the quality of your posture.

Sitting or standing in a slouched position with the shoulders hunched forward, head slumped and heart closed will always affect your ability to breathe deeply.

By simply lengthening the spine, you naturally begin to lengthen the breath.

Rolling your shoulders back and down opens your heart and creates a clear passage for a big heartfelt inhale, taking oxygen deep into the lungs.

Maintaining good posture throughout the day takes concentration and self-awareness at first but, over time, you'll find it becomes a natural state.

cleanliness *is* next to godliness

Purity – shaucha in Sanskrit – is an important part of yoga. It is one of the niyamas or inner disciplines identified by the father of yoga, Patanjali, in his eightfold path to living a good life.

Specifically, shaucha relates to cleanliness in every part of your life: Externally – in terms of your house, car, office space, clothes; physically – your body; internally – eating pure clean natural foods; and mentally – where positive, kind, considerate thoughts are the gateway to liberation.

It also extends to the air we breathe. Next time you go to the ocean or travel to the mountains, notice how your breath naturally tends to slow down and deepen as your body savours the clean, sweet air.

When I was teaching yoga in Hong Kong, living in a highly polluted city and working all day in air-conditioned studios, I noticed how the quality and depth of my breathing diminished. Almost subconsciously, it seemed, I was breathing faster and less deeply.

I realised that my body's natural defence mechanism had kicked in to protect me from the pollutants and toxins I was inhaling.

When you find the right place to practice your deep breathing and meditation, make sure the air is clean and pure.

If you meditate at home, choose a well-ventilated room where the air is always fresh. Alternatively, you may prefer to practice by the sea or sitting beneath a tree on a riverbank or in a pocket of rainforest, close to the source of pure oxygen released by all that lush vegetation.

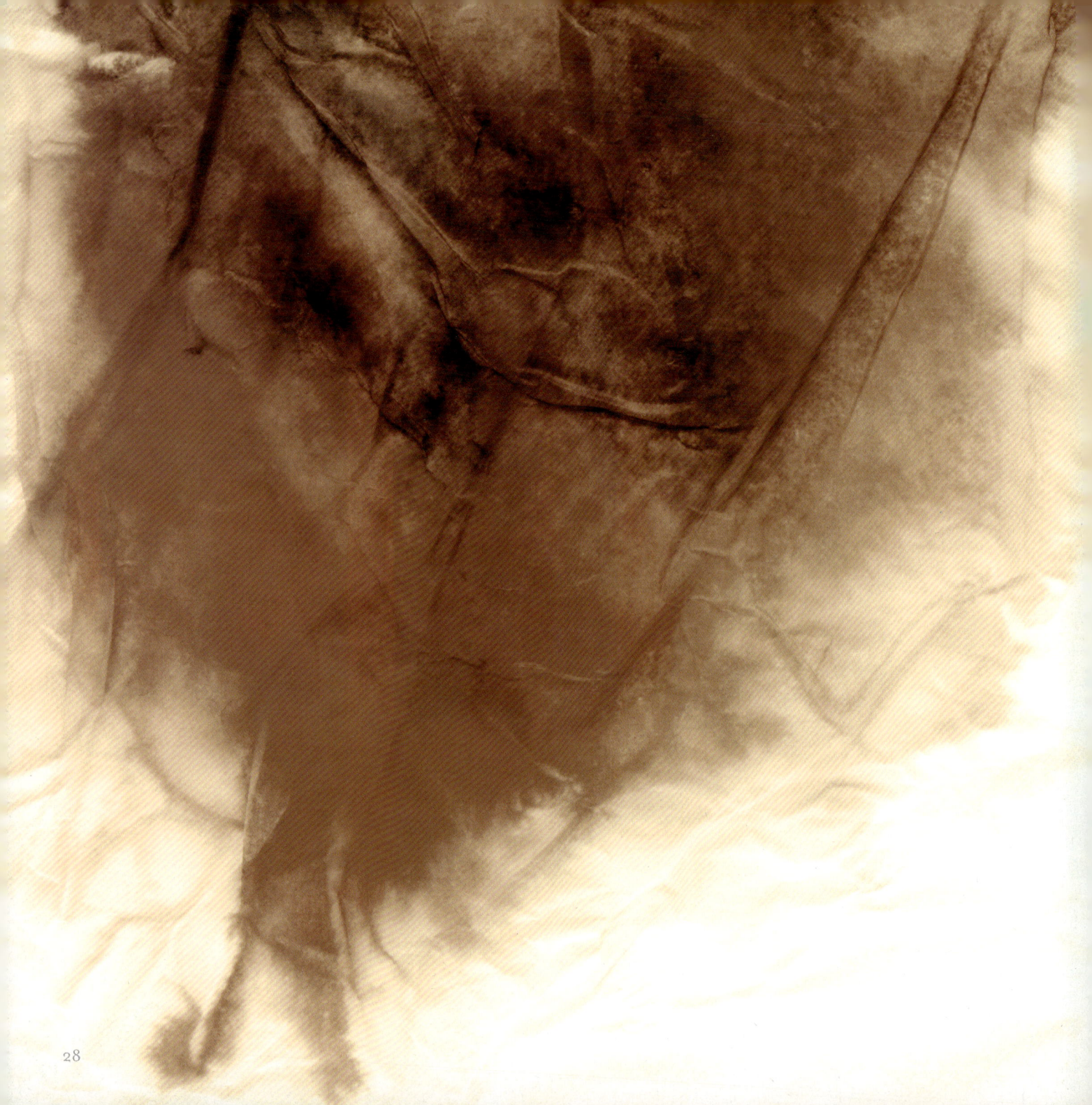

our own personal air-conditioner

In yoga, we breathe in and out through the nose.

There are a number of very specific reasons why we do this.

First and foremost, the nose is perfectly structured to filter and purify the air we take into our bodies: Our sense of smell allows us to detect any pollutants or odours to ensure we are in a safe, clean environment; the fine nostril hairs trap any dust or bacteria from the atmosphere; and the mucus membranes catch anything that manages to get past those first two lines of defence.

Breathing through the nose also helps to slow down the respiratory rate. It's like sipping a drink through a straw – much, much slower than opening your mouth and sculling it down your throat!

The nostril cavity has the most amazing ability to heat the air before it reaches our lungs.

Try this simple exercise: Take a deep breath through the nose and notice how sweet the air is as it slips down the throat. Now take a deep breath through your mouth. Can you feel how cold and harsh the air is on the back of your throat? You'll probably need to swallow to get rid of the dryness.

The lungs find it easier to absorb air when it's warm. This absorbed air, in turn, delivers life-giving oxygen to the bloodstream, helping to release the muscles and loosen the joints in preparation for your yoga practice.

the picture of health

Studies have shown that slowing our respiratory rate and taking longer, deeper breaths brings a whole range of health benefits.

These days, doctors and psychologists often prescribe breathing techniques – even yoga and meditation – to patients presenting with a wide range of dis-eases, from stress, anxiety and depression through to heart problems.

In one research project, a group of cardiac patients were taught 'complete yogic breathing' and practiced breathing at around six breaths per minute for an hour a day. At the end of the month, researchers found that those patients were breathing more slowly, had higher levels of blood oxygen and performed better on exercise tests.

When we inhale, we draw oxygen into the lungs which then travels to the heart and the bloodstream. The heart pumps that oxygen-loaded blood to every part of the body where it, in turn, seeps into every tissue and bone cell.

The deeper and more slowly we inhale, the more oxygen we can bring into the lungs and heart and blood and body. It improves our circulation, blood pressure and the health of our faithful heart; all of which will improve our overall health, life expectancy and quality of life as we get older.

The regular practice of deep, slow, conscious breathing will also affect our mental processes.

Just think about it: When we see a friend getting angry and upset, what do we say to them? "Stop, walk away and take ten deep breaths."

And that's not just an old wives' tale: Anger management therapists commonly recommend and teach deep breathing practices as a highly effective technique for anger control.

According to medical researchers, there is a wealth of similar mood-altering benefits to be gained from the regular practise of a few simple breathing techniques.

Deep slow breathing will help you focus, relax and sleep at night. It improves concentration, focus, organisational skills and decision-making. It aids clear functioning and self-control. It reduces stress, tension and temper, bringing an overall feeling of serenity and peace of mind.

Simply becoming more aware of the breath and the effect it has on the body can create a change in consciousness.

An even breath, it is said, reflects an even mind … and vice versa.

However perhaps most importantly, our breath is the link between body, mind and spirit – the lifeforce that connects our outer, physical self to the always-present inner self.

The great yogic teachers believe that the spirit travels into the body when we inhale and leaves as we exhale … with every breath we take.

It is our connection to the world around us and to the great universal energy force.

We inhale the air that the trees have purified for us and we breathe out all the toxins, negativity and ill-will that can so easily build up inside our bodies.

When we breathe into every cell of our body and let that lifeforce ignite our inner flame, we can then shine brightly on the world around us.

the complete yogic breath

Inhaling and exhaling … slowly, deeply … through the nose … we are now ready to master the complete yogic breath.

If we're slouched over the computer at work, racing through our daily tasks our breathing tends to become short and shallow. It is when we are busy and unconscious that we tend to limit ourselves by only drawing air into the upper chest and lungs.

If we employ a straight spine with our hearts open, our breathing becomes much deeper, travelling down into the lower lungs forcing the abdomen to rise and fall.

What we need to remember is that the lungs are a round sphere shape and in order to maximise our lung capacity we must breathe into the sides and back of the body to achieve our full breath potential.

The complete yogic breath is a combination of this high, low and middle breathing.

Breaking it down into a four-part numbered sequence:

1. Draw the breath deep into the lowest part of the lungs, feeling the abdomen and diaphragm expand.

2. Continue filling the air into the mid-section, expanding into the sides of the ribcage.

3. Push the air into the back of the lungs, feeling your shoulder blades press against the back of the chair or into the floor.

4. Feel the air spill up into the collarbone and shoulders.

On each inhale, draw the air into your lungs in the order of stage 1 > 2 > 3 > 4. On the exhale, empty the lungs in the order of 4 > 3 > 2 > 1.

In this way, the complete yogic breath is not just deep breathing. It is the deepest possible breathing.

pranayama

Way back in the second century BC, one of the very earliest yoga practitioners and teachers, Patanjali, set down a series of guidelines on how to live a meaningful and purposeful life.

His eight-fold path is called ashtanga – a Sanskrit word which literally means 'eight limbs' (ashta – eight; anga – limb). Together, these 'limbs' serve as a prescription for moral and ethical conduct and self-discipline; directing our attention to our health and helping us to acknowledge the spiritual aspects of our nature.

Pranayama is the fourth anga. Translated from Sanskrit as lifeforce (prana) control (yama), yogis believe that it not only rejuvenates the body, but actually extends life itself.

Within the practice of ashtanga yoga, pranayama is broadly defined as the correct technique for breathing. It can be practiced as an isolated exercise by sitting quietly and simply focussing on the breath or it can be integrated into our daily yoga routine.

Pranayama breathing techniques are said to provide a wide range of health and wellness benefits:

Massaging and exercising our internal organs – lungs, heart, diaphragm, abdomen, intestines, kidneys, pancreas – through the movements created by deep breathing;

Improving blood circulation to every part of the body by maximising the amount of oxygen drawn in with each breath;

Improving the overall health of our heart through increased oxygenation;

Increased lung function and elasticity of lung tissues which ultimately increases our fitness and energy levels.

Pranayama is also beneficial in controlling key health issues such as obesity, hardening of the arteries, back aches, headaches, stiffening muscles and joints, rheumatism, hypertension and more.

Through the regular practise of pranayama, you will start experiencing a 'lightness of being' and a sense of inner peace. You will sleep better, have better concentration and have more energy for life.

You will feel as if there are springs fitted to your feet!

four stages of pranayama

In pranayama, the breathing practice is divided into four stages:

1. **Inhalation – puraka**
   The process of drawing air in through the nose in a single, smooth and continuous movement.

2. **Full pause – abhyantara kumbhaka**
   Stopping the flow of air and holding it in the lungs in complete stillness.

3. **Exhalation – rechaka**
   Relaxing the muscles to force the air out of the lungs and through the nose in a single, smooth and continuous movement.

4. **Empty pause – bahya kumbhaka**
   Stopping the flow of air and keeping the lungs empty in complete stillness.

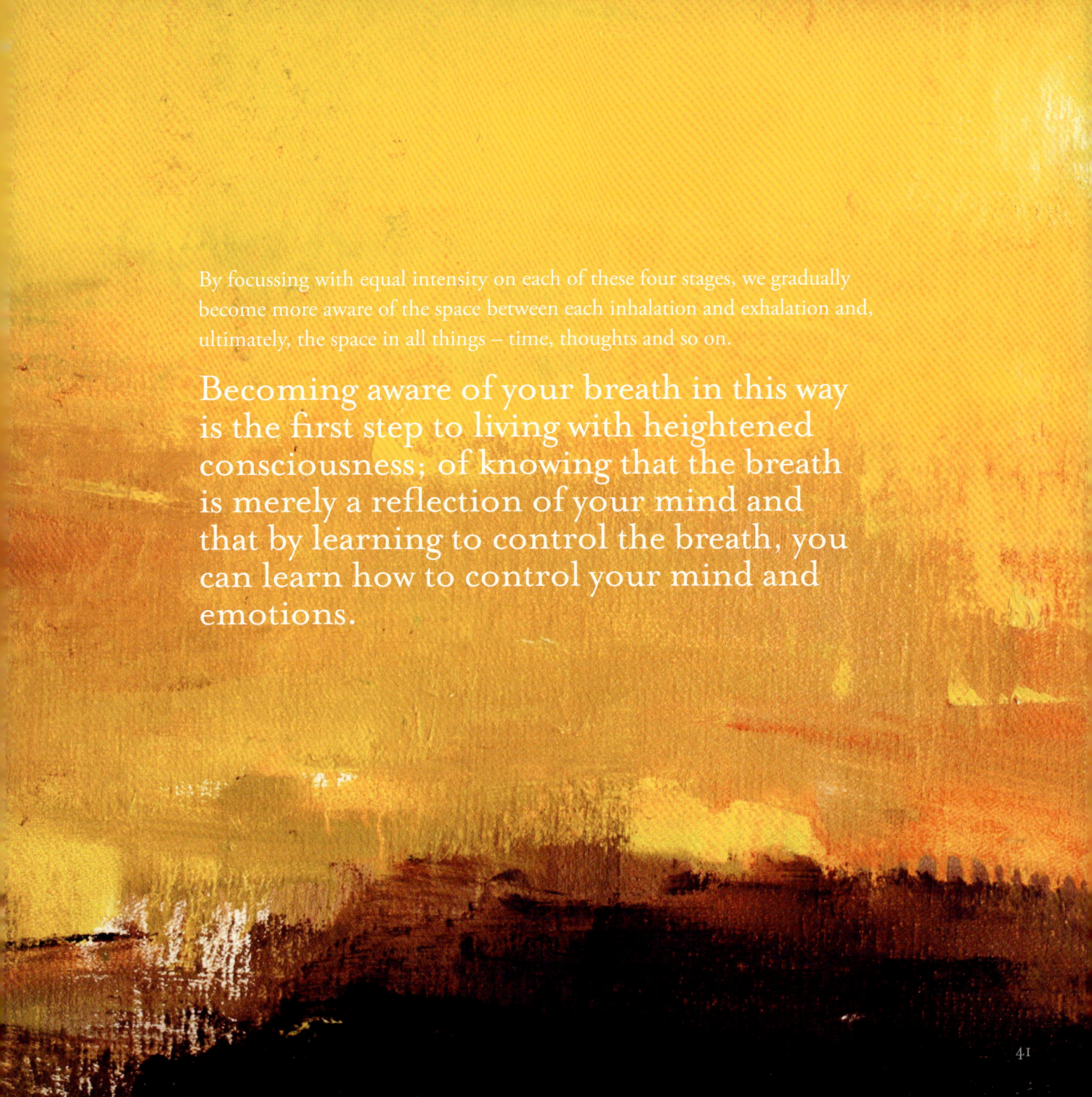

By focussing with equal intensity on each of these four stages, we gradually become more aware of the space between each inhalation and exhalation and, ultimately, the space in all things – time, thoughts and so on.

Becoming aware of your breath in this way is the first step to living with heightened consciousness; of knowing that the breath is merely a reflection of your mind and that by learning to control the breath, you can learn how to control your mind and emotions.

capturing the lifeforce

Bandhas are a technique used in pranayama to capture and lock the lifeforce into specific energy channels within the body.

In hatha yoga, there are three main types of bandhas:

Jalandhara Bandha – chin lock or throat lock
Tuck the chin in towards your chest and push your tongue up against your palate to focus prana on the visuddha chakra, located within the throat.

Uddiyana Bandha – abdominal lock or flying-up lock
Exhale completely and pull the abdomen in and up under the ribcage to focus prana on the manipura chakra in the solar plexus. This bandha provides additional support for the spine, increases core strength and delivers a deep massage to the internal organs.

Mula Bandha – root lock
Engage the perineum to lift the pelvic floor and focus prana on the muladhara chakra at the base of the spine. Using this bandha on the inhale creates internal lift and a sensation of lightness throughout your yoga practice.

—

Maha Bandha – the triple lock or great lock – is a combination of all three bandhas applied during an empty pause in the sequence of chin lock, abdominal lock and root lock; and released in reverse order.

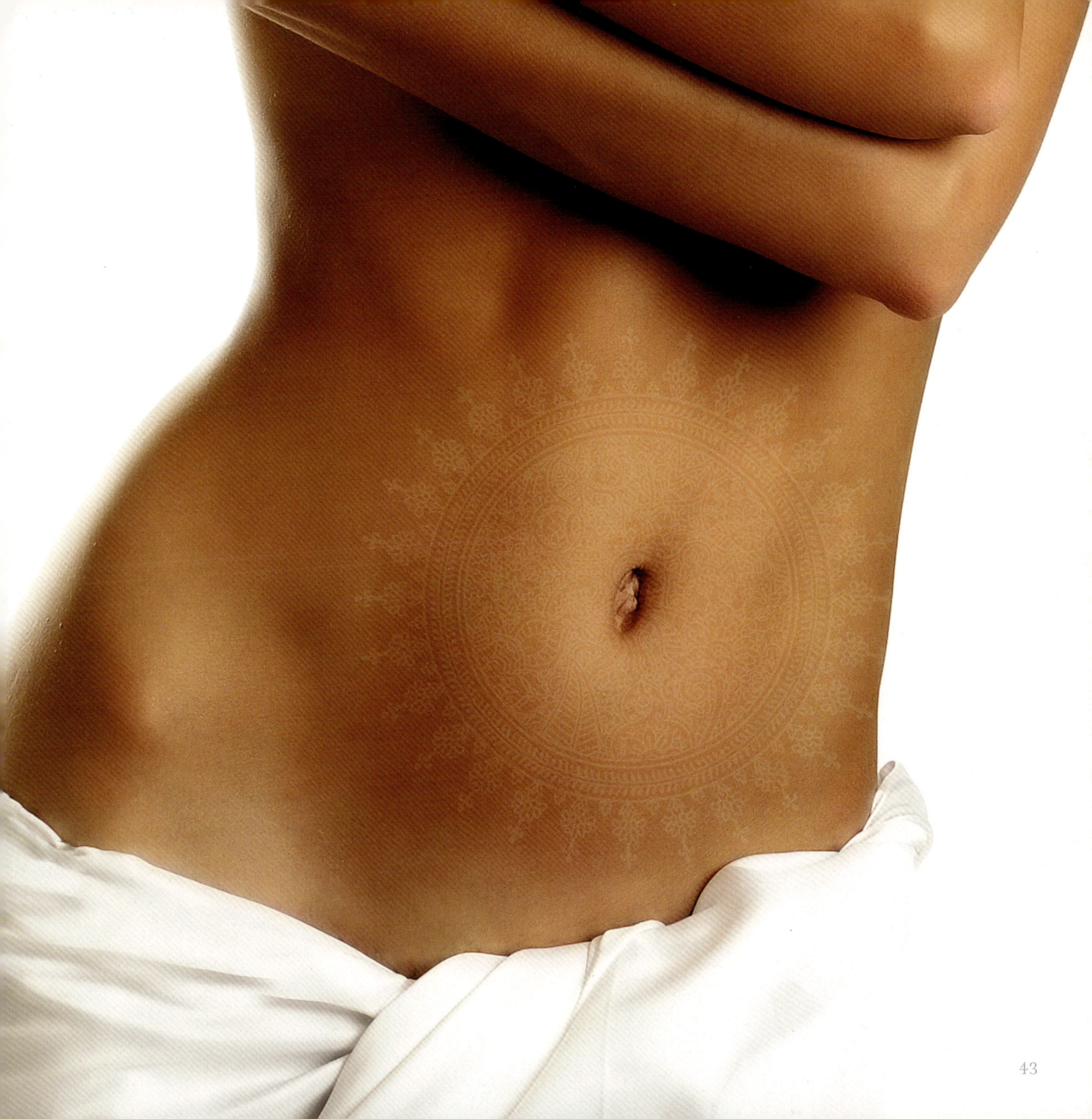

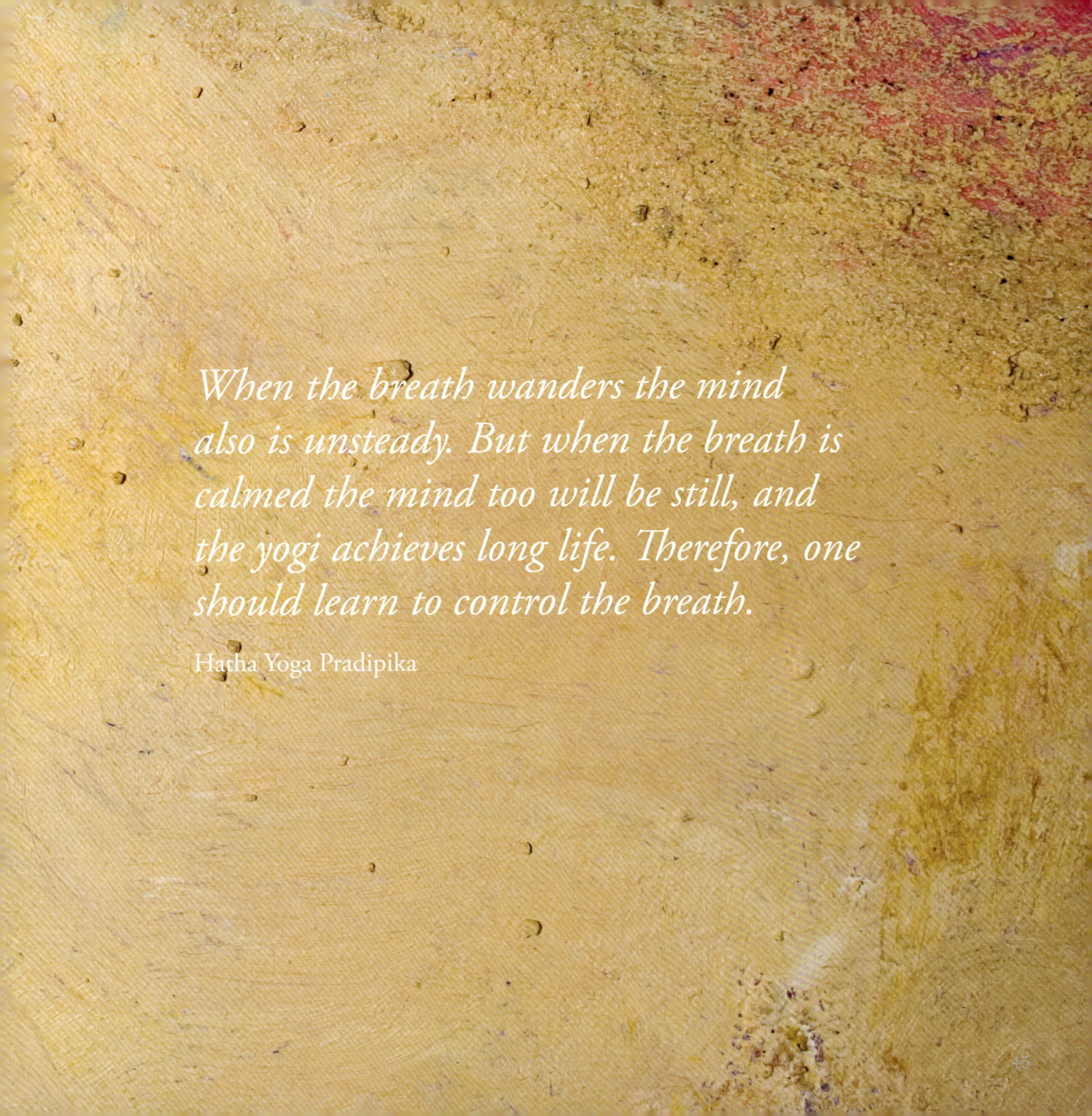

When the breath wanders the mind also is unsteady. But when the breath is calmed the mind too will be still, and the yogi achieves long life. Therefore, one should learn to control the breath.

Hatha Yoga Pradipika

haaa is for 'happy'

Ujjiya is an audible breathing technique that intensifies the breath and increases the flow of oxygen into the lungs and bloodstream.

Basically, it involves contracting the glottis in the back of the throat to create an extended 'haaa' sound.

Think about what happens when we squeeze a hose: the waterflow becomes more concentrated and powerful as it moves through a smaller opening. This is exactly how the ujjayi breath works to maximise the body's intake of oxygen.

Ujjayi also has a number of other benefits: It heats the body internally, allowing the muscles to move more freely, particularly in some of the extreme poses; and the sound drowns out any distracting chatter going on in your mind, refocussing your attention on the breath.

In a yoga class, we are encouraged to practice ujjayi pranayama (which loosely translates as 'power over mind') throughout the entire practice. The regular, paced 'haaa' sound sets the rhythm, serving as a metronome as you move seamlessly from one pose to the next with an even uninterrupted breath.

To create the ujjayi breath

- Hold your hand up in front of your face and breathe out through the mouth, making a long 'haaa' sound – just as you do to clean your glasses. Notice how warm the air is? Can you feel that spot of vibration it creates on the back of the throat?

- After practicing this a few times, close your mouth halfway through the exhale and expel the rest of the breath through the nose while still creating the 'haaa' sound.

- Now focus on that vibrational spot at the back of the throat and continue making the 'haaa' sound as you inhale and exhale through the nose. Make sure the 'haaa' always comes from the back of the throat – not the nose; they are completely different sounds. It's also important not to over-emphasise the 'haaa' so that it sounds angry or aggressive. It should all be smooth, rhythmic and effortless.

Whilst ujjayi is quite difficult to master at first, with practice it will become second nature. The truth is that you can tell an advanced yoga practitioner by the quality of their ujjayi breath – not by the quality of their moves!

pranayama techniques

Over the millennia, pranayama has been developed into many different styles, each with its own unique benefits. There are pranayama techniques designed to heat the body, cool the body, balance the central nervous system, detoxify the body, clear the mind … the list goes on and on.

Some of the techniques are quite advanced and should only be practised under supervision or by experienced, qualified yogis. The techniques included here, however, are quite suitable for all levels of ability and should give you plenty of ideas for varying your breathing practice.

sukha pranayama

Sit comfortably in any meditative posture – sitting upright in a chair or cross-legged on the floor is best. Lengthen the spine, rest your palms gently on your knees and observe your natural breathing. Feel the breath flowing in and out of the lungs. Let the breathing be natural. Feel the abdominal movement – expanding out as you inhale; contracting inwards on the exhale. Keep your mind clear and simply 'observe' the breath. Visualise power and energy flowing into the body each time you inhale; see tension, stress and dis-ease exiting the body on the exhale.

Benefits

- Provides deep relaxation to the body and mind

- Strengthens the nervous system and respiratory system

- Improves concentration

- Relieves stress, depression and hypertension

sheetali pranayama

Sit comfortably in any meditative posture. Lengthen the spine, bring the thumbs and index fingers into gentle contact and rest your palms on the knees. Draw out the tongue and roll it up from both sides to form a tube-like opening. Slowly suck the air through it and fill the lungs completely. After full inhalation withdraw the tongue and close the mouth. Hold the breath for some time before slowly exhaling through the nose. Repeat for as long as desired.

Benefits

- Useful in treating fever

- Good for liver, spleen and blood purification

- Reduces tension and high blood pressure

- Cools the nervous system

dirgha pranayama

Sit comfortably in a meditative posture with your spine erect, or lie down on your back. Start by taking long, slow, deep breaths through the nostrils.

Step 1: Inhale for three counts, drawing the breath deep into the lower lungs and feeling the belly expand. Hold for two counts.

Step 2: Inhale for a further three counts, drawing the breath into the mid-chest region and feeling the rib cage open outward to the sides. Hold for two counts.

Step 3: Inhale for another three counts, allowing the breath to fill the upper lungs into the chest and clavicular region.

Step 4: Exhale for nine counts and repeat.

Benefits

- Promotes proper diaphragmatic breathing

- Relaxes the mind and body

- Oxygenates the blood and purges the lungs of residual carbon dioxide

nadi shodhana

Sit comfortably in any meditative posture. Lengthen the spine and close your eyes. Using the right thumb, gently press against the right nostril to block the airflow and inhale slowly through the left nostril until your lungs are completely filled. Release the right nostril and use the ring finger of your right hand to close the left nostril. Exhale slowly and completely through the right nostril until your lungs are completely empty. Keeping your index finger in position, inhale though the right nostril on the next breath and exhale through the left nostril. These two complete breaths comprise one round of Nadi Shodhana Pranayama.

Benefits

- Cleanses and tones up the entire nervous system

- People suffering from coughs and colds benefit greatly

- Heart is strengthened

- Blocked nostrils are cleared

- Removes mental tension and worries

- Induces a feeling of peace

the energy seals

The distinctive yoga hand gestures known as mudras or 'energy seals' have been practised for thousands of years. They are said to rebalance the body's energy by reconnecting our electro-magnetic currents and are believed to help cure many diseases.

Traditionally, each finger represents one of the five elements

Thumb	-	**fire / agni**
Index	-	**air / vayu**
Middle	-	**ether / akash**
Ring	-	**earth / prithvi**
Little	-	**water / jal**

The most common mudra practised in yoga is the gyan mudra, where the index finger and thumb pads are gently connected while the other three fingers extend outwards.

In this position, the index finger is said to symbolise the ego – the individual self, me, I; and the thumb symbolises the divine universal self. When the ego humbly bows down and reconnects to the universal self, we are realigning our source energy – no longer separated or detached but a part of the whole.

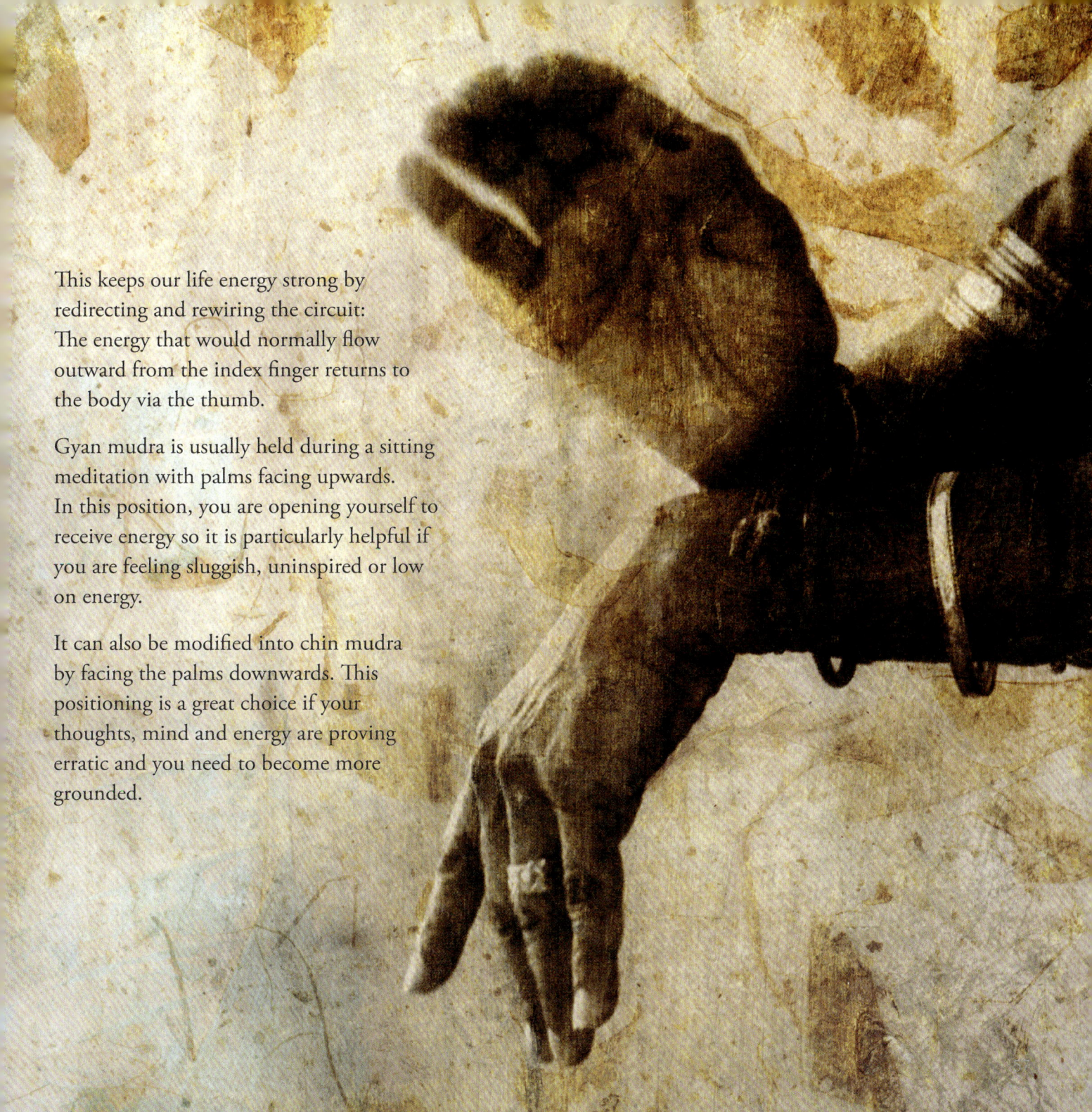

This keeps our life energy strong by redirecting and rewiring the circuit: The energy that would normally flow outward from the index finger returns to the body via the thumb.

Gyan mudra is usually held during a sitting meditation with palms facing upwards. In this position, you are opening yourself to receive energy so it is particularly helpful if you are feeling sluggish, uninspired or low on energy.

It can also be modified into chin mudra by facing the palms downwards. This positioning is a great choice if your thoughts, mind and energy are proving erratic and you need to become more grounded.

finding your stillness

Pranayama practice is a meditation in and of itself. Focussing all your attention on the breath moving in and out of your body is the perfect way to empty the mind of the day's worries and distractions.

For an experienced practitioner, the inhalation – hold – exhalation – hold sequence becomes automatic after the first few breaths and your mind settles into the stillness of meditation.

If you are relatively new to the practice of pranayama, you may need to make a conscious delineation between breath awareness and the meditative state.

Meditation can be done anywhere at any time, but it's probably best to establish a routine of sitting in stillness at the same time every day.

For many people, first thing in the morning is ideal. Your mind is slow and quiet and you haven't yet been caught up in what the day might bring.

Start by finding your seat. The optimum position for meditation is to be seated in an upright position – either in a straight-backed chair or cross-legged on the floor. Lengthen the spine and rest your hands gently on your knees.

Now close your eyes down and be still. Don't move or fidget no matter how restless or itchy you may feel – that's just your mind trying to take over.

Listen to the breath moving in and out of your nostrils. On each inhalation, take the air deeper and deeper into your lungs until you are doing the complete yogic breath. Feel how that all-encompassing intake of oxygen affects the body physically and let your awareness travel further inwards.

Many people find that the chanting of mantras – a single sound, word or phrase – helps them along the journey into that deeper meditative state. Repeating the mantra over and over trains your mind to focus and brings a deep feeling of calm as the sound reverberates through your energy channels.

You can choose a Sanskrit word, such as aum – the sound of all creation – or shanti – peace; or you may prefer an English phrase that has particular meaning to you. 'Breathe in love; breathe out compassion' is one I often use.

As you feel yourself sinking deeper and deeper, you will naturally fall into silence and simply 'feel' the mantra vibrating internally.

Just breathe...

Practicing pranayama and meditation for 20 minutes every day is the very best gift you can give yourself. After just one week, you will begin to see a profound change in yourself. You will feel more centred, content and at peace; inspired and energised.

Over time, regular meditation helps you clarify the core essence of who you are and what is truly important in your life.

living meditation

On my first yoga teacher training course, I asked one of the other students what meditation meant to her.

After only a moment's consideration, she answered: "For me, meditation is how I hang the washing on the line or clean the house or prepare a meal for my family.

"It's about being totally present in everything I do and turning it into a sacred experience."

I was totally blown away. Wow! What an amazing way to live your life!

I've since learnt that this 'living meditation' - being in a highly conscious state as we go through our daily tasks and routines – is a truly beautiful practice.

Admittedly, it's hard to maintain 24/7 – but we can all try living meditation at certain moments of the day.

Buddhist monks, for instance, practice 'walking meditation'. Timed to the breath, each and every step is taken with acute awareness. Lifting … bending … stretching … placing each foot. Feeling the deep connection to Mother Earth. Being grounded to the planet. Living totally in the moment.

There is no rush. no thought.
just experiencing each moment as if it was eternity.

For me, surfing is a magical living meditation. Sitting alone out there on my
board as the sun peaks above the horizon. Timing my breath to the gentle
rise and fall of the waves. Feeling the coolness of the water on my hands and
legs like silk to the touch. And if I'm really lucky, the universe will send an
albatross, dolphin or even a whale to share my sacred solitude.

I've also found you can practice living meditation simply eating a meal.
I start by focussing on the smell, flavour, texture of each mouthful, feeling
the sensation as the food moves across my tastebuds. Then there's the energy
created by all the muscles in my jawline and throat as I chew and swallow
slowly to extend the experience. It's like you're eating for the very first time
in your life.

Imagine how your life would change if you could just be aware and present
in every moment. To breathe in the fresh, sweet air. Smell the perfume of
the flowers. Hear the birds singing. Look up to the clouds. Let go of your
thoughts and just breathe.

In such a moment, there is absolutely no room for negative thoughts and
unhappiness.

the sleep of the yogis

Yoga nidra – the sleep of the yogis – takes the breathing-meditation sequence one giant step further.

Whilst the actual state of yoga nidra is universal and timeless, the techniques for arriving at what has been described as the 'psychic sleep' date back to 1880 and were originally handed down from guru to disciple within the Indian religions.

In yoga nidra, you actually leave the conscious state, go through the dream state and into the deep sleep state … and yet remain fully awake.

There is no guided imagery; no exploration; no effort whatsoever to be aware of any object or any part of your body or being.

You let go of any words, thoughts, images or impressions.

The mind is completely empty. Silent. Still.

In yoga nidra, you complete that sequential process of moving inwards: From the body to the breath to the mind until you finally empty into the conscious deep sleep of nothingness… and everything.

moving meditation

The connection between the movement of the breath and the movement of the body into asanas (yoga positions) was profoundly inspired by Sri Krishna Pattabhi Jois.

Practising yoga from the age of 12, Pattabhi Jois established the Ashtanga Yoga Research Institute in India in 1948.

The vinyasa yoga system he popularised aligned movement and breath; turning static yoga positions into a continuous dynamic flow.

Using a multitude of postures seamlessly linked by the breath creates a 'moving meditation'. In this harmonious dance between the breath and the body, the yoga practitioner becomes the musician, playing multiple chords to trigger vibrations deep within the energy chakras and inspiring all those who are blessed to be in the presence of such in-tune grace.

Do your practice and all is coming.

Sri K Patthabi Jois

bend

bend

Through the practice of yoga asanas,
we balance body, mind and spirit;
realigning our energy and clearing
the obstacles that stand in our way

Hatha yoga detoxifies the body physically, mentally, emotionally and energetically.

As you develop a regular asana practice, you'll find that you naturally begin to change the way you eat. Day by day, you'll become more aware of how food affects the body: what foods make you feel high in energy and ready to conquer the world; and what foods make you feel sluggish and lazy.

Without even having to think about it, you'll want to start eating better. It becomes a subconscious positive choice rather than a conscious negative decision to deny your body of what it thinks it wants by going on a diet.

You'll eat less and less and feel lighter and lighter. Charged with vitality and energy, you'll be able to cope with whatever physical, mental or spiritual challenges your life presents.

the lightness of being

A lot of people seem to think that, if they can't twist their bodies into a pretzel then they can't do yoga.

Nothing could be further from the truth.

The real reason we practice all the different yoga positions is to prepare our body to meditate in complete stillness for extended periods of time.

Sitting in the traditional lotus position, anything longer than five minutes can feel like a lifetime. It requires a strong and flexible body – and that's just to get into the posture! If your muscles and joints are tight and stiff, you'll be too busy focussing on your aching knees, screaming back muscles or painful hips to focus your mind on silence and finding that inner tranquillity.

And so, we 'bend'.

Hatha yoga was developed by Yogi Swatmarama in the 15th century and is the system practised most commonly in the Western world today. The series of physical postures called asanas (Sanskrit for 'seat') is all about creating balance in body and mind: Balancing the left and right side of the body; balancing strength and flexibility; and balancing our internal energy channels.

Even the name itself – hatha – represents balance: Between the sun (ha in Sanskrit) and moon (tha) or, more correctly, between the solar and lunar energy channels in our body.

from left

From a general health and wellness perspective, the hatha yoga asanas address a wide range of issues:

- The asana movements increase blood flow to the digestive tract and stimulate intestinal action so that digestion becomes more efficient;

- Enhancing overall strength and flexibility has been consistently shown to relieve and prevent back pain;

- Yoga's slow-motion movements and gentle pressures reach deep into troubled joints to relieve arthritis;

- Studies conducted at yoga institutions in India have reported impressive success in improving asthma;

- The relaxation and exercise components of yoga have a major role to play in lowering and preventing high blood pressure;

- Studies have shown that yoga can relieve the symptoms of a range of other illnesses including arteriosclerosis, chronic fatigue, diabetes and obesity.

...to right

Most people favour one side of the body over the other. From our earliest days of childhood, we instinctively and consistently use our right or left hand for most tasks – writing, throwing, lifting, pushing.

Over the years, that 'favoured' side naturally becomes either stronger or more flexible than the other.

When you first start practising yoga, you'll probably find that it's easier to balance on one leg as opposed to the other, or that you can twist further on one side.

The challenge is to develop equal range and stability on both sides.

Improving this left-right balance plays a vital role in maintaining good physical health throughout our lives and most particularly as we get older.

Studies have shown that the most common injuries for elderly people occur due to lack of balance: Slips, trips and falls can be devastating for seniors, often resulting in permanently reduced mobility.

My older clients often tell me how much they have benefitted from their regular yoga classes. They feel stronger, have an increased range of movement and are more steady on their feet. By maintaining a fit and flexible body, they feel like they can still live a life filled with choices.

Learning to go with the flow

In western society, we tend to work linearly in a straight line from A to B. Eastern cultures have a more abstract approach – jumping from A to M then back to D to arrive at B.

If you've ever driven in Asia, you'll totally understand what I mean! Drivers don't seem to pay any attention to traffic lanes or road signs, ducking and weaving between cars, trucks, pedestrians and wandering animals with no clear pattern that we can see.

For us westerners – so accustomed to structure and rules – it looks like total madness.

Yet it seems to work. There are relatively few accidents in Asian cities, compared to the number of vehicles on the roads. If you can take a deep breath and relax, you'll see that there is an intuitive flow that Asian drivers instinctively tune into as they 'feel' their way through the flow of traffic

The same can be said for life in general: Take a deep breath, relax and be prepared to be flexible. We don't always have to travel from A to B by the fastest straight line possible; sometimes the journey is more interesting and pleasurable if we let the flow take us in and around the obstacles and challenges.

strength & flexibility

When yoga first started becoming popular in Western societies, it was generally regarded as the domain of super-flexible lightweights: Pixie-sized woman and turban-wearing beanstalks who might be able to wrap their legs behind their heads but would probably be toppled over by the slightest puff of wind.

These days, anyone who has been to a dynamic yoga class will tell you that there is a lot of strength required.

Over the years, I have taught big, burly footballers, storemen, construction workers and the like. They may look sceptical when the classes begin with some basic breathing exercises but by the time we've worked through our sun salutations, warrior poses, backbends and abdominal curls, they are a lather of perspiration and their faces scrunch up with the sheer effort required to hold each position.

Complementing that aspect of physical strength is the focus on stretching and increasing flexibility of all the different muscles and joints – especially those muscle groups that are not involved in everyday movements.

The key to developing flexibility through yoga – or any other exercise system for that matter – is to understand that it's all about YOUR body … not the body of the person next to you!

They may very well be able to get their head to their knees in a forward fold or rest their third eye on the floor in a seated yoga mudra – particularly if they've been practicing yoga for many years.

But the fact is that you will get the same stretch by taking your body to its own maximum. If that means your head is still several centimetres away from reaching your knees in that forward fold, so be it. Enjoy that feeling of lengthening and stretching; move just that little bit further on the next exhalation … and know that next week you'll be able to achieve even more.

Remember, too, that the strength and flexibility we develop through our regular yoga practice is just as much about the mind as it is about the body.

As our muscles and joints become stronger and more flexible so too does our attitude to life.

Being flexible is all about being open and adaptable to change when life throws you a curve ball. We are all headstrong when it comes to our likes and dislikes – from the food we eat and the music we listen to through to the clothes we wear.

All of these things are completely normal and quite okay! Yoga is not about changing your personality or telling you how to live your life.

But when it comes to a challenge like coping with the loss of a loved one, having to change careers or even something simple like a lack of food choices to suit your dietary requirements, having the flexibility to see things from a different perspective and the strength to stand up for your core beliefs will allow you to live in harmony with others … and with yourself.

balancing the energy channels

We all have those days when we feel low …
sluggish … unmotivated … can't be bothered.
Or when we're totally charged … high on life …
able to leap tall buildings in a single bound.
(Okay – so maybe that's a slight exaggeration but
you know what I mean!)

It seems to change for no reason – from one
extreme to the other.

Eastern medicine has a very logical explanation for
this and it's all about the invisible energy channels
running through our body.

Does that sound a bit 'off the wall'? Try this
experiment: Rub your hands together rapidly for
about 30 seconds or so. Now place them a few
centimetres apart.

Wait for it … Can you feel it? … It's like there's a
cushion of air vibrating between your palms. Try to
push your hands together very gently. Can you feel
that slight resistance?

That's your own personal power source at work;
the energy force that the Indians call prana and the
Chinese call chi.

This energy is constantly being circulated through
the body through a series of channels or nadis (the
Sanskrit word for 'tube' or 'pipe').

Some ancient texts say that we have more than
72,000 nadis in our body. They intersect at the
chakras lining our spinal column and transport our
life force energy out to the extremities and beyond.

The three most important nadis are the lunar ida
(yin in Chinese philosophy) of the left side which
is associated with feminine attributes; the solar
pingala (yang) of the right side, associated with our
masculine attributes; and the central sushumna
running from the base of the spine to the crown
of the head.

It is along the sushumna that we find our seven
main chakras. Coming from the Sanskrit word
for 'wheel', the chakras are believed to spin in a
clockwise direction moving energy up and down
the spine.

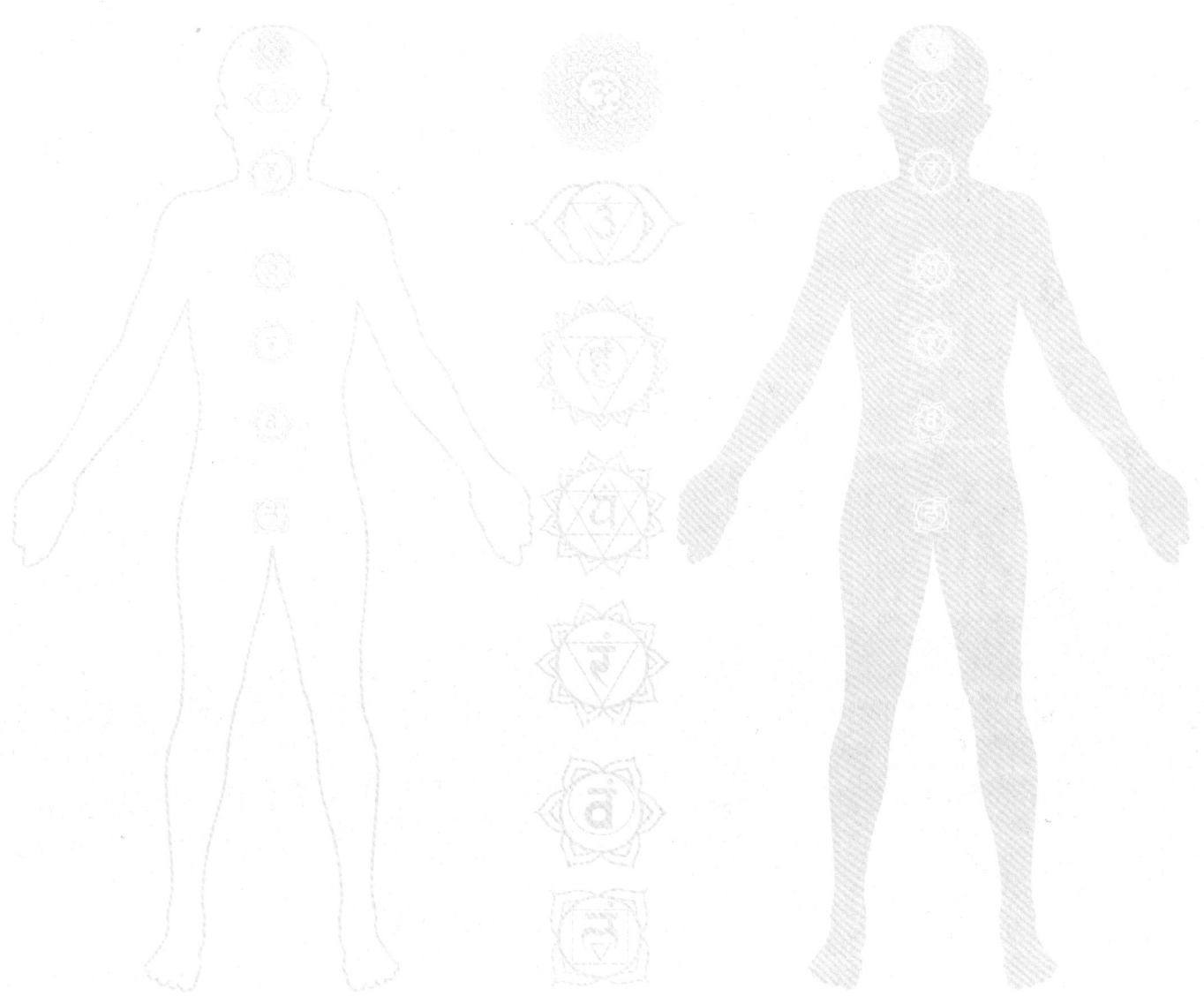

the sacred chakras

Eastern medicine practitioners believe that those low and high levels of energy we all experience at different times are directly related to our chakras. When we feel slow and sluggish, our chakras are blocked up with stagnant energy. When we're running around at 100 miles an hour, the chakras are too open and we run the risk of crashing and burning.

The name 'chakra' comes from the Sanskrit word for wheel because they are believed to spin in a clockwise direction at various speeds and work together in harmony like the cogs of a wheel.

Each chakra is also said to vibrate at a different frequency which is, in turn, related to the individual colours of the light spectrum.

In a physical sense, each chakra relates to specific emotions and organs of the body. When they are blocked or too open, those organs don't operate efficiently and effectively; thereby causing dis-ease and adversely affecting our general well-being.

Each sequence of poses – standing, backbending, forward folds and so on – focuses on specific chakras, working to clear any blockages, rebalance our energy and realign its internal flow.

In addition to maintaining good health, a clear energy flow allows us to have a clear mind which, in turn, allows us to open and channel our divine intuition so we can achieve anything our heart desires.

sex versus love?

Men and women may not be from different planets but they certainly can be worlds apart when it comes to how they view love and sex. For men, sexual energy is primarily a physical response while for women, it is much more of an emotional experience. This could very well be because a man's sexual organs are located in the first – root – chakra while in a woman, they're located in the second – sacral – chakra.

root chakra
muladhara

'I have'

The muladhara or root chakra is located at the base of the spine and is related to our basic needs for survival, safety and security. When the muladhara is blocked, we feel fearful, anxious, insecure and frustrated. We find it hard to stand up for ourselves and may feel victimised or experience a sense of not belonging. Eating disorders are often related to this chakra, as well as physical ailments such as constipation, gastric upsets, weak bones and knee problems.

sacral chakra
svadhisthana

'I feel'

Located five centimetres below the naval, the sacral chakra governs our sexuality, creativity, intuition, self-worth and nurturing instinct. As such, it relates to a wide range of emotional issues, including our ability to get along with others and go with the flow. Physical issues stemming from a blocked svadhisthana include kidney problems, painful menstrual cycles, lower back pain, urinary tract infections and, occasionally, addictions.

solar plexus chakra
manipura

'I can'

The centre of the abdomen is the source of our personal power – the pace of ego, passions, impulse, anger and strength. When the manipura is open and clear, we feel able to take on the world, facing new challenges with joyful enthusiasm because we are confident of our place in the universe. Physical problems associated with blockages of this chakra include poor digestion and liver function, diabetes, nervous exhaustion and food allergies.

heart chakra
anahata

'I love'

The anahata is the central chakra, forging the connection between the body, mind and spirit, guiding our intuition, hope, love and forgiveness. It is from here that we find our ability to love ourselves and others. When this chakra is out of balance, we feel sorry for ourselves, paranoid, indecisive, unworthy and afraid of getting hurt. Physically, it impacts on the heart, lungs, circulatory system, shoulders and upper back.

throat chakra
visuddha

'I speak'

The throat chakra is all about communication: what we say and how we express our creativity through thought, speech, singing, dancing, art and the written word. It is here that we find our ability to speak the truth and express who we are without fear. Interestingly, visuddha translates as 'purification'. Physical ailments related to a blocked or out-of-balance throat chakra include thyroid problems, skin irritations, sore throat, ear infections, teeth grinding, hearing difficulties and stuttering.

third eye chakra
ajna

'I see'

Ajna means 'beyond wisdom' or 'the centre of perception' – hence the reason we focus on this central point in the forehead just above the eyes during meditation. This is where we tune into our higher selves, getting rid of our attachment to all things material and using visualisation, intuition, imagination and sometimes even telepathy and clairvoyance to see the truth.

crown chakra
sahasrara

'I know'

The crown of the head is our point of connection with the Divine, where the energy of mind and body joins with our spirit and flows out to the universe. Focussing on this chakra allows us to draw in wisdom and knowledge to gain a deeper, even cosmic, understanding of our personal beliefs and our place in the world. If you suffer from migraines, depression, frustration and unexplained exhaustion, balancing the energy of sahasrara may be the answer.

bend & stretch

One of my teachers once said to me that the limitations of your body are the physical manifestation of the limitations of your mind.

As we gradually bend, stretch and open our bodies through the yoga poses, she said, we are also bending, stretching and opening up our minds and, ultimately, our lives.

To put this in more concrete terms – yoga is not just about being able to bend backwards or stand on our heads; it's about being compassionate, centred, caring and considerate of others.

We can start this process by being compassionate, caring and considerate of ourselves in our yoga practice.

Relax. Soften. Let the body unfold gently and gradually.

As you hold each pose, feel the muscles lengthening and opening as you breathe in. Visualise your breath – your energy – your life force – moving into that muscle and easing away any pain so that you can twist or fold or bend just that little bit further as you breathe out.

When I see students with their faces all screwed up, looking as though they're about to pass out from the effort, my favourite instruction is: "Face of an angel! Smile!"

Softening and relaxing your face reminds you to soften and relax your body to let it open gradually.

Think of it like the curious child, eager to see the lotus flower in full bloom. Pulling open the petals before they are ready to unfold naturally will simply break the petals and damage the flower.

This is exactly what happens when we don't practice the art of patience with ourselves. We push our bodies before they are ready and end up causing damage.

In theory, yoga can never hurt you. It's actually impossible! In practice, however, we break our own precious bodies by pushing and straining and going too far. Our ego takes over and we end up hurting ourselves.

Survival of the most adaptable

Charles Darwin may have claimed that evolution is based on the survival of the fittest but the truth is that it has much more to do with the survival of the most adaptable animals.

Over the millennia, different species adapted by developing gills, legs, wings and fingers - physical features that would enable them to live through natural disasters and out-last their predators.

Just like history has shown us, our physical, mental and spiritual survival depends on being adaptable; bending our beliefs, ideas and views as new opportunities and adventures present themselves.

Because, let's face it, we never know what the universes may have in store for us.

Our physical, mental and spiritual survival depends on being adaptable

the sacred harmonic

A traditional yoga class commences with a series of deep breathing exercises, followed by the chant of 'aum'.

Aum – or 'om' as it sometimes written – has no literal translation; it is simply all-encompassing.

Used in a class situation, it becomes a deep, rolling vibration that unites the group's collective energy and creates a harmonious sacred space for the ensuing practice.

Chanted on your own, it rolls up through the spiritual chakras – from the heart to the throat to the third eye to the crown – igniting the flame that burns within and connecting your lifeforce to the energy of the universe.

There are four distinct parts to the aum mantra, each of which should be held for equal duration:

- **A** – starts in the heart centre. Place your hand on your chest and you can literally feel the vibrations within. The mouth should be wide open to create the complete sound.

- **U** – centres on the throat chakra. Move you hand up here to feel the resonance. Purse your lips slightly to make a round open-whistle shape.

- **M** – the final audible stage moves through the third eye and up to the crown of your head. Place your hand here and feel how your entire skull vibrates with energy as you press your lips together for the 'mmm' sound.

- **Silence** – this last stage is absolutely essential and totally magical! Listen as the vibrations melt away and sit in stillness to absorb the true essence of the mantra.

After silence, that which comes nearest to expressing the inexpressible is music.

Aldous Huxley

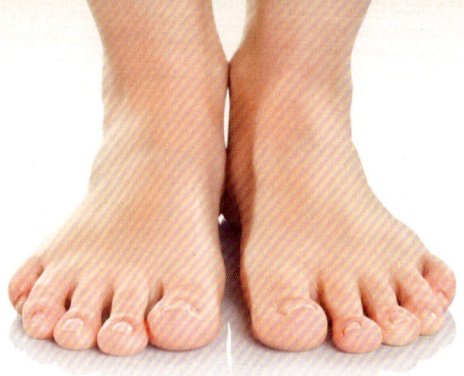

looking beyond infinity

In yoga, we use drishti to help us achieve focus. Literally translated as 'perception', it refers to the point where your gaze rests as you move through the asanas.

The most common drishti is the tip of the nose (nasagrai drishti). Letting your gaze rest there softly during balancing or standing poses turns your attention inwards and aids stability.

Other traditional drishti include the third eye (for meditation and breathing), upwards (as you move your head up in backward bending poses), the hand (side stretches), the naval (downward-facing dog) and the foot (forward folds).

My teacher would take this concept a step further and say the drishti is the doorway to self-realisation. It's as if you look beyond the point of focus to the depths of infinity where you will find oneness by becoming the point of focus.

moving in sequence

In each yoga class, you will move through a range of different poses and postures: standing, balancing, backbending, twisting, core strengthening, forward folds, hip openers, inversions.

Each series of movements has its own potency, causing the body's energy to vibrate through the chakras at different frequencies.

As such, there is a logical order in which to progress from one pose to the next so as to stretch, strengthen and bend every muscle, joint and energy channel in a harmonised sequence.

yogic breathing | pranayama

Your yoga practice should always start with the breath; drawing oxygen deep into the abdomen, rib cage, back and collarbone to set the rhythm for what is to come.

Our ultimate aim is to maintain that complete yogic breath throughout the practice, timing your movements like the waves washing in and out across the sand or the wind gently moving the branches of a tree back and forth.

As you settle the body into the different positions, make a conscious effort to lengthen and open the muscle as you inhale and apply an extra effort to twist, bend and stretch just that little bit further into the pose as your lungs empty on the exhale.

When your mind starts to wander – as it does for all of us – return your focus to the breath, visualising how its movement through the body loosens our muscles, frees our joints and massages our internal organs allowing us to maximise the stretch in each pose.

sun salutation | surya namaskar

The sun salutation sequence is over 2500 years old and is dedicated to Surya, the Hindu sun god.

The Hindus believe that the sun – Surya – is the visible form of God that we can see every day. In the ancient Veda texts, the sun is also praised for enhancing good health and prosperity.

So there are plenty of good reasons for starting our asanas with surya namaskar, which is traditionally practiced facing the sun.

There are many different versions of the sun salutation but it usually comprises a series of twelve movements designed to stretch every muscle in the body, with each position counteracting the one before. The sequence must be performed at least twice, leading with the right leg during the first series and the left leg during the second.

The most important aspect of the sequence is to synchronise the breath with the movements: Inhale on the backward bending postures and exhale on the forward folds to create a flowing, seamless pattern where the body and breath are as one.

The sun salutation prepares the whole body for the rest of your practice; stretching and lengthening all the major muscle groups, warming the body, elevating the heart rate, and regulating the breath, while creating a sense of inner connection and balance.

The Hindus believe that the sun – Surya – is the visible form of God that we can see every day.

standing poses

Tadasana – the mountain pose - is said to be the foundation for all of the other poses you will move into throughout your practice.

Standing poses generally are considered to be the most heating. They use the largest muscle groups – the legs and buttocks – and therefore require more energy which, in turn, generates more heat throughout the body. Consequently, you will actually burn more calories in standing poses than sitting.

Whenever you move into a standing posture, it is paramount that you build the pose from the base up. Imagine that you're erecting a skyscraper – the most important thing is to make sure you have a good strong foundation.

Start by distributing the energy evenly across the feet. I love the visualisation of wearing roller skates where you have to oh-so-carefully balance your weight equally on all four wheels.

The internal lift of the body rises from the arch of the foot, travelling to the outer ankles, knees, quadriceps, pelvic floor (mula bandha) and lower abdominals (uddiyana bandha). The heart lifts. The neck extends. And finally the energy elevates to the crown of the head.

In addition to improving your stamina and building strength, standing poses help you to find stillness – of the body and mind. They require intense concentration and focus which benefit so many aspects of your daily life.

balancing poses

Whilst balancing poses are commonly linked with standing poses, they actually encompass balances for the arms, as well as the legs.

This series is designed to balance the right and left sides of the body; equalising strength and flexibility to improve our overall stability. A lot of women, for example, have strong legs but are weak in the arms. A holistic yoga practice incorporates poses to build this upper strength so that our bodies are balanced throughout.

On a physical plane, improving our balance has obvious health benefits in terms of preventing slips, trips and falls that can be quite damaging, particularly as we get older.

From a mental perspective, however, the challenge of maintaining these poses is often a reflection of what's going on in our busy minds.

As you move through the balancing sequence in your yoga practice, you'll almost always fall out of a pose as soon as your thoughts start to wander.

The secret of mastering balance is to be truly present in the moment; focussing on building a strong, steady connection with the earth.

As you shift your weight from one side to the other and settle into the pose, visualise the energy flowing up from the ground and into your feet or hands like the nutrients flowing from a tree's roots and up into the trunk, branches and right out to the tips of each leaf.

One of my favourite verses from Patanjali's yoga sutras that I like to quote during the balancing sequence is sthira sukham asanam: May my connection to the earth be steady and joyful.

Yes, I know: A yoga pose is often far from 'steady', let alone 'joyful'! But the aim of our practice is to establish that strong firm connection to the earth where the earth represents everyone in our lives and all those relationships that bring us joy.

And don't forget: While many balancing poses are quite simple, they can all be made more advanced in an instant, just by closing your eyes.

backbending poses

Backbends are not just about the back.

To feel the full benefit of these poses, you actually have to open the entire front of your body – the thighs, ankles, hip flexors, abdominals, chest, shoulders, throat.

As such, on an energetic level, backbends relate to moving into our future – with openness, energy and love.

I've found that many students are quite wary about doing backbends – even frightened sometimes. I wonder if this means that they are fearful of what the future may hold for them?

But I can tell you than when you abandon the fear and achieve that first big backbend you will feel absolutely amazing.

Backbends stimulate the entire nervous system and energise the heart, throat and solar plexus chakras. They will leave you buzzing all day. In fact, one of my teachers says that you should never do intense backbends at night because you may not be able to sleep.

There are different types of backbends to suit all levels of ability but you do need to be careful not to overwork the spinal column. Doing backbends, forward folds, backbends, forward folds one after the other will wear out your back.

To open up and loosen this area, you need to gradually intensify the postures and neutralise the spine by following your backbends with the twisting poses and finishing with forward folds.

twisting poses

Twisting is my favourite part of the yoga practice. I lace lots of twisting poses into my classes – combining them with standing postures, balancing postures and even sitting postures.

The spine actually moves in four directions: forwards, backwards, sideways and into a twist.

This final movement flexes and strengthens the spine which, as we know, is the first area to degenerate with age. In India they have a saying that you are as old as the flexibility of your spine … so keep twisting!

Most importantly, twisting also massages all the internal organs.

In the lower back region, the movement works beautifully on the colon, squeezing out all the toxins built up from stress, tension and eating the wrong foods.

Always remember to twist to the right side first. This delivers that massage to the ascending colon to loosen and dislodge all those toxins. The left-side twist then massages the descending colon to squeeze them out of your system.

As we loosen and squeeze out those toxins, visualise how we are also loosening and squeezing out any negative thoughts, emotions and beliefs we may be carrying around.

Inhale to lengthen the spine; exhale to twist and try to hold that position for a minimum of five breaths as we let go of all the baggage that no longer serves us.

forward folding poses

Just as backbending poses relate to moving towards the future, forward folds are all about looking back into the past. As we fold and close the body, we get the rare opportunity to look deep inside our soul and reflect on who we are and how we have come to be.

Students who are new to yoga often feel claustrophobic in intense forward folds. The secret is to focus on opening the back of the body, completely relaxing and letting go of the calves, hamstrings, buttocks, back and neck.

That tightness you feel in the hamstrings relates to anger and frustration. Elongating and slowing down the breath will elongate the muscles and loosen this area – in the same way that we "take a deep breath" to take the edge off our anger.

In seated forward folds, it's usually the hips that restrict our range of movement. The hips relate to our sexuality and creativity. They take longer to open up because we don't use these muscles as often as others.

You should never force the hips open by pushing too hard. Allow them to open naturally, in their own good time, just like the lotus flower opens to the morning rays of the sun.

There's no rush. We have the rest of our lives to fold and unfold. And if it doesn't happen in this lifetime, we always have the next!

core strengthening poses

Being a devoted Pilates teacher, as well as a yoga instructor, I'm an advocate for developing a strong core centre. This group of muscles in our lower abdomen is critical to everything we do. It supports and protects the delicate spinal column and is essential to all the twists, forward folds and backbends, as well as maintaining our balance.

Studies also say that excess abdominal fat is linked to diabetes, respiratory problems and heart disease and that if you have a trim, healthy waistline, you are less likely to develop cancer and chronic illnesses.

But perhaps even more importantly, our core centre is the source of our self-esteem, inner strength and courage.

Seated deep in this area of the body is the manipura chakra – the city of jewels. Next time you find yourself struggling through the core strengthening postures of your yoga practice, try visualising this beautiful treasure chest of sparkling exotic jewels that need to be safeguarded and cherished.

inversion poses

Inversions turn our lives upside down, giving us a new perspective on life.

So often, we get caught up doing the same things, the same way, day in, day out. Flipping upside down into a headstand or shoulder stand gives us the opportunity to see things from a new angle and experience life differently; finding new ways to flow through our journey.

Being a yogi is all about being open to change and accepting other points of view that may not be the same as ours. Over time, regular inversions can change our core values and beliefs as we look at the world from a different perspective and become willing to try new things.

For the physical body, turning upside down causes fresh blood to flow through the organs and gives the lower limbs a well-deserved break from the hard work of constantly pumping blood back up to the heart.

Inversions are particularly good for water retention, varicose veins, spider veins and cellulite but should be avoided if you are pregnant or menstruating.

relaxation | savasana

The relaxation period at the end of your yoga practice is not meditation. Whereas meditation is a mental exercise best practised sitting upright, relaxation is a distinct pose: savasana – the corpse pose.

According to the legendary yogi, B K S Iyengar, savasana is the hardest of all the poses to master. Students will often fall asleep or can't relax because they're itching to rush out and get back to the hustle and bustle of their everyday life.

But it is during savasana that the body truly absorbs all the goodness of the yoga practice. When the external body is finally still and completely relaxed, the energy stimulated by the asanas is pulsating through all the internal nadis and chakras. You can almost feel the cells dancing as you lay back and soak in the sweet sensations that the practice creates.

It is in this safe place that our body, mind and spirit can heal and draw strength from all that balancing, bending, twisting and inverting.

You should always allow at least seven to ten minutes for relaxation at the end of a one-hour yoga practice. If you have more time, fifteen minutes is even better.

It is extra nice if you have some props: a bolster or blanket placed under the knees will help release the back and an eye-bag will stop any light filtering in so you can sink deeper into the abyss.

Different teachers will have different ways of helping you to relax into the pose. Some will use body mapping, working up from the toes to focus on releasing every joint and muscle; others may guide you through the colours of the chakras; while some find visualisations helpful.

Whatever method works for you, this is your time to block out the world and experience on the deepest level all the goodness that yoga brings to your life.

finding your inner guruji

There are many different styles of yoga to choose from, each one suited to different personalities and levels of ability.

The key is to try as many as you can until you find a system – and a teacher – that resonates with you. It's a bit like looking for a new hairdresser or doctor – you just have to find the right fit.

Above all, remember that you are your own best teacher. You know exactly how far you can go in any given pose on any given day.

The aim is to find the guruji that shines within each and every one of us.

Teachers open the door, but you must enter by yourself.

Chinese Proverb

blossom

blossom

As a flower bud slowly blossoms bringing beauty to the garden so, too, do we take the lessons of our yoga practice to bring joy to the world around us

blossom

It's all well and good to practise your pranayama breathing techniques on a daily basis and be able to master the most challenging asanas in your yoga class, but how does this make a difference in your everyday life? How does that help the people around you or make the world a better place?

One of my yoga teacher training students put it beautifully:

"Yoga helps me see things more clearly," he said.

"If our soul or spirit is a lake, the mind – our consciousness – is the wind that causes the waves and ripples; chopping up the smooth surface and churning sediment from the bottom to make the waters muddy and murky.

"Yoga has the power to calm the breeze. The lake becomes still and clear so that I can see right through to the very depths of my spirit.

"It's only when we have this clarity that we can see our true passion and create the pathways to fulfil our life's purpose."

This is what I call 'blossoming'.

My own analogy is that, when we 'breathe' and 'bend', we are like a tightly closed bud; nurturing ourselves internally and building our strength so that when we open and 'blossom', we can truly contribute to the beauty of the world around us.

in the fullness of the blossom, the true magic of yoga is finally revealed in what we present to the people we love, the community that surrounds us and the planet that serves as our home.

patanjali's eight limbs of yoga

Throughout the centuries, the great yogic masters have embraced the practice of yoga as a life philosophy. In his famous Yoga Sutras, Patanjali formalised this philosophy in the 'Eight Limbs of Yoga', providing a clear set of guidelines to living your best life.

1.   Yamas

The first limb addresses our core ethical standards and sense of integrity. Based on the golden rule, 'Do unto others as you would have them do unto you', Patanjali listed five key yamas.

Ahimsa – Non-violence

Not just in a physical sense but also in our words, thoughts and deeds. We can relate ahimsa to so many aspects of life – from how the food we eat is prepared through to how we treat the planet.

Satya – Truthfulness

Being true to ourselves and true to others. First and foremost, satya requires us to know and understand our authentic self so that we can be honest and clear in our relationships with others.

Asteya – Non-stealing

Again, this relates to a whole range of issues beyond the obvious definition of stealing someone else's property … which most of us would never contemplate. When we take credit for someone else's work or present their ideas as our own; when we take someone's place in a queue or dart into the parking space they were waiting for; when we waste someone's time or draw on their energy to make ourselves feel better … these are all violations of asteya.

Brahmacharya – Sexual restraint

Whilst the classical translation of brahmacharya is 'celibacy', for most of us it means being faithful in a monogamous relationship; devoting our sexual energy to one partner at a time; not indulging in indiscriminate sex simply because it makes you feel good momentarily.

Aparigraha – Non-greed

The fifth yama leads to a life of beautiful simplicity where we eat only what our body needs to survive; where we don't fill our homes with unnecessary material possessions; where we share our wealth and skills and knowledge freely with others.

2.   Niyamas

The second of Patanjali's eight limbs deals with self-discipline and spiritual observances.

Shaucha – Purity

Cleanliness of mind, body and environment. Being mindful of our thoughts and deeds: are they kind and directed to helping others? Paying attention to our bodies through good nutrition and maintenance of our health, as well as basic showering, washing our hair and cleaning our teeth. Ensuring our home, workplace and the environment is free from dirt and clutter.

Santosa – Contentment

Being happy with what we have and not envious or resentful of others because of what they may have. Finding joy in the simple beauty of every day.

Tapas – Austerity

I like to relate austerity to discipline: The consistency of working towards our goals; making a commitment to all those things that improve our lives – whether that be a daily walk on the beach or a course of study or our regular yoga classes.

Svadhyaya – Study of self

Devoting time to the understanding of who you really are deep down inside. In meditation, silence, stillness and 'alone time', you will slowly but surely come to discover your authentic self.

Ishvara Pranidhana – Surrender to the Divine

Ishvara pranidhana literally translates as 'giving up or surrendering to God', but for those who don't subscribe to a theistic belief system, it can just as easily be interpreted as connecting to the universal energy flow or having faith that all is unfolding as it is meant to be.

3.   Asanas

The physical postures practised in yoga – the asanas – are Patanjali's third limb. In the yogic view, the body is the temple of the spirit and caring for this temple is an important part of our spiritual growth. Through the practice of asanas, we develop physical strength and flexibility, mental discipline and the ability to focus … all of which are vital to achieving the higher states of consciousness defined in the final four limbs.

4.   Pranayama

The fourth limb – our breathing practice and control of the life force – is the connection between the internal attributes governed by the yamas, niyamas and asanas and our forward journey into the external spiritual realm.

5.   Pratyahara

Our first step towards spiritual enlightenment is the 'withdrawal of the senses'; making a conscious effort to detach ourselves from the outside world and all its stimuli. By closing down our external senses of sight, smell, hearing, touch and taste, we can then look inward – observing ourselves objectively and shining a light on all those thoughts, actions and habits that are detrimental to our health and stunting our inner growth.

6. Dharana

Dharana – or 'concentration' – flows on from the withdrawal of the senses and challenges us now to focus on a single mental object with unwavering attention. By focussing on a specific energetic centre in the body, an image of a deity, the silent repetition of a sound or even gazing into a candle, we are able to empty every other thought from our mind in preparation for deep meditation.

7. Dhyana

Dhyana is the pure state of meditation where that one point of focus identified in dharana fades away and leaves us with … nothingness.
The mind is totally still with no thoughts, no distractions and no awareness of the outside world.

8. Samadhi

And finally, we reach samadhi – the state of ecstasy. Here, 'nothingness' becomes 'everything' as your energy – your spirit – connects with the universal life force that resonates through all living things. Patanjali described the completion of the yogic path as "the peace that passeth all understanding" – the ultimate goal that surely all human beings aspire to.

While Patanjali's eight-limbed path may appear to be a difficult or even impossible goal to achieve, remember that yoga is a journey. We may never achieve samadhi or even dhyana, for that matter but every stage along the pathway brings an abundance of goodness and benefits into our daily lives which we, in turn, share with others as we blossom.

Yoga is 99% practice and 1% theory.

Sri Krishna Pattabhi Jois

getting to know 'you'

From Patanjali's eight limbs of yoga, we can see that the asanas – the physical practice of yoga – is really only a small part of the whole.

The real power of yoga is how you apply it in your daily life.

Before you can take your blossoming self out into the world, however, the very first relationship you have to nurture is your relationship with yourself.

The regular practice of asanas, pranayama and meditation opens up our energy channels and allows us to see ourselves more clearly. It's like switching on a light to dispel the darkness … or, perhaps more accurately, slowing turning up a dimmer switch that gradually illuminates your authentic self.

As in any relationship, it will take some time to get to know this person. What makes you happy? What are you good at? How can you make a contribution to other people's lives?

Sometimes, that first question is the hardest: Do you really know what makes you happy?

It's easy to see what doesn't make us happy: We don't like our job. We don't know what to do with ourselves on weekends. We're not satisfied in our relationship. We're too fat, too thin, too short, too tall.

We spend hours, days, weeks focussing on what we don't like about ourselves and our lives.

Imagine if we turned that around and devoted all that time to thinking about what we do want in our lives.

Don't like your job? Start thinking about what you would like to do. What was your passion as a child – did you like drawing or writing or dancing or singing? Were you good at maths or science? Did you love going to the beach or walking in the bush or curling up with a good book?

As children, we instinctively identify our strengths and weaknesses. We know exactly what makes us happy or sad. And yet somehow we lose this clarity in the process of becoming an adult and taking on adult responsibilities.

Maybe it's time to get back in touch with that inner child and ask him or her what they would like to be when they grow up. Make a list of all those interests and talents and skills and see if you can't translate them into a more fulfilling and satisfying career.

Sometimes, that first question is the hardest: do you really know what makes you happy?

Don't know what to do with yourself in your spare time? Go back and check that inner child list again. If you can't create a financially viable career out of those childhood passions, I'm sure you will at least find a hobby that will replenish your spirit.

Enrol in painting classes. Join a writers' group. Audition for an amateur theatre production or a choir. Take piano lessons. Volunteer to help out at the library. Not only will you find satisfaction in doing what you love, I guarantee you'll find a whole load of new friends with similar interests.

Not satisfied with your relationship? I'm sure you can come up with a long list of what annoys you or bugs you about your partner. But how about giving some thought to what you do want in your relationship. More time together? More meaningful conversations? More connection? More intimacy? What can you do to bring those positives into the relationship?

Or perhaps there's nothing you can do to repair the rift. Perhaps you've learnt all you needed to learn from this relationship.

So maybe it's time to move on – to be on your own, at least for a while so you can rediscover who you truly are and what you want from life.

And as for that dissatisfaction with your physical attributes – first and foremost, be honest: Are you really too fat or too thin … or have you got caught up in the magazine images of what constitutes the 'perfect body'?

Go and see your doctor for an honest assessment of whether your weight is truly unhealthy … and believe what they tell you!

If the answer is that you need to lose weight, set a realistic, healthy goal and make a conscious decision to eat better and exercise more. If you need to gain weight, sign up for a gym program that will help you build muscle.

Of course, the 'too tall' or 'too short' scenario brings to mind the most important lesson of all. To paraphrase the famous Serenity Prayer: May you have the serenity to accept the things you cannot change; the courage to change the things you can change; and the wisdom to know the difference!

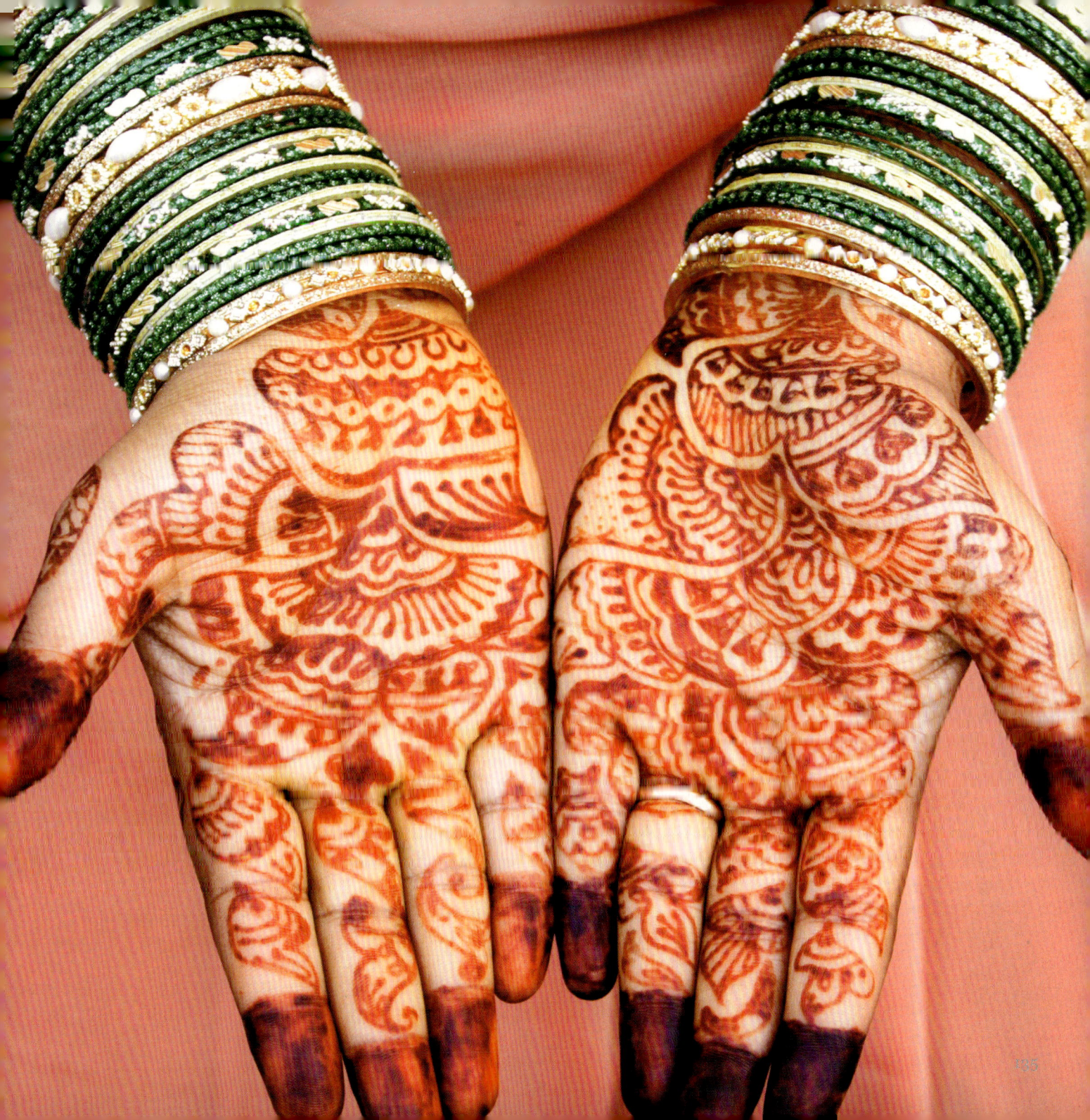

make it happen

Knowing what you want – what makes you happy – is the first step towards creating the life that you want. The next step is working out how to make it happen.

There are lots of imaginative ways to do this. Sometimes it really is as simple as writing your goals on a piece of paper.

Just remember to be very specific: Do you want to write a book … or do you want to write a book and have it published? Rather than saying vaguely that you want to 'lose weight' … work out exactly how many kilos you want to lose.

Pin your list somewhere so you'll see it every day – on the fridge or on a wall near your desk. Look at it regularly and remind yourself what you want to achieve.

If you need a little more direction or if you have some really big goals on that list, you may like to plan out your journey in more detail. Set smaller, interim goals that you can easily accomplish in the short term and celebrate your progress as you achieve each milestone.

Personally, I prefer the colour and impact of a 'vision board'. The one hanging in my office is covered with pictures and notes that in some way illustrate my hopes and dreams and desires.

I use a white board so I can easily make changes and adjustments as I achieve one goal and create new ones.

Sometimes I change direction completely – and that's perfectly okay. In fact, that's half the fun of being open and flexible!

In the words of Walt Disney, "If you can dream it, you can do it". The only thing that can stop us is our limiting beliefs – our negative self-talk.

Think about what you are saying to yourself: You'd be no good … you'd be taking too much of a risk … you'll probably fail.

If your best friend came to you with an idea they were really excited about, would you ever, ever say: "Don't do it. You'll be hopeless. It's too risky. You'll never make a go of it."

Of course not! You wouldn't dream of speaking to a good friend like that … so why on earth do you think it's okay to say those things to yourself??

Imagine if you didn't care whether you succeeded or failed; that you just wanted to have a go. How much fun would that be? What a ride! And who knows where it might take you.

Win or lose, you will have set your life on an exciting new path. If it doesn't turn out as you hoped, you will certainly have gained the skills and knowledge to try again; and if it does work out …

Wow! Look out world!

there's no-one else like you

Throughout this all-important exercise of defining
and designing a life of fulfilment, always remember
that you are unique.

This is not about being a cardboard cut-out of
some image you think you should aspire to. It's not
about exuding the same love and acceptance that
you might admire in your yoga teacher, or giving
selflessly of all your time to charity, or having the
patience of a saint.

There are thousands – hundreds of thousands – of
flowers in God's garden. From sunflowers to tulips
to daffodils and daisies, each one adds to the beauty
of the whole.

So blossom as your own flower —
quirky, distinctive and totally, authentically YOU.

Your beliefs become your thoughts,
Your thoughts become your words,
Your words become your actions,
Your actions become your habits,
Your habits become your values,
Your values become your destiny.

Mahatma Gandhi

a circle of friends

True prosperity comes from having special people in our lives; people who genuinely care about us and want to grow with us.

With a clear, authentic understanding of who we really are, we're now ready to create honest, loving, lasting relationships with the most important people in our lives.

When we are content with ourselves and living our passions, we naturally attract people who are on the same wave-length. They recognise the twinkle in our eyes, the openness of our smile, the spring in our step.

Nurturing these relationships is easy and organic: You can speak honestly and openly; you give and receive from each other equally; you can deal with issues as and when they arise because you both have the ability to act from love.

Other relationships – with family members, workmates, the driver who cuts you off in the traffic! – can be a little more challenging.

When I get caught up in stewing about how other people or situations are affecting me in a negative way, I know that I'm acting from my 'small self'. It's my ego that's saying "My life sux" or "so-and-so is not doing the right thing by me".

What I have come to realise (after many, many years of coaching!!) is that this is just my story; my interpretation of the truth – possibly based on something that's happened to me in the past or on some other issue that might be worrying me.

If I can step out of my small egotistical self, I can understand that these 'annoying' people each have their own 'stories'. They may have misinterpreted the intention of what I've said or done; they may be in a hurry to pick up a child from school; or they may have to answer to a demanding boss. We all bring our different 'stories' to any given situation.

And maybe it'll make you think twice before you instinctively react in anger or with hurt feelings or by taking it personally when someone's thoughts, words or actions don't align with yours.

In fact, everything in our entire existence is just our 'story' – our interpretation of events. Nothing is really 'real'.

Makes you think, doesn't it?

And maybe it'll make you think twice before you instinctively react in anger or with hurt feelings or by taking it personally when someone's thoughts, words or actions don't align with yours.

143

nurturing relationships

Stepping out of our ego or 'small self' is the first step to building better relationships.

The second challenge is to think about how our interactions with those people in our lives can make them feel better about themselves.

I have a few simple guidelines that really work in my life:

1. Be genuinely interested in other people

People are endlessly fascinating. They all have something interesting to share … if only we're interested enough to listen. We can draw people out by asking the right questions and listening actively to their answers. Don't create barriers by crossing your arms or legs. Lean slightly forward and maintain eye contact. Keep the focus on them and don't jump in with responses that will redirect the conversation to back to you.

2. Be mindful of the power of words

When it's your turn to talk, make sure your words will benefit the other person. Will they feel special, important, happy, welcome, comfortable, safe, non-intimidated and good about themselves from what you have to say?

3. Be humble and open to learn

Everyone has their own tales of struggle, challenge, trial and triumph, and the way they've dealt with their obstacles may very well help you deal with your own. Just think about it for a minute – almost everything we learn in life, we learn from other people. How many lessons – big and small – did you miss out on today by not listening to what someone had to say?

4. Give praise, compliments and gratitude

You have the incredible power to make someone feel good about themselves with a simple word of praise or thanks. Remember how great you felt the last time someone said: "Wow – you've done a fantastic job on that project" or "I really appreciate your help" or even something simple like "you look beautiful in that outfit". The good vibrations can last all day, giving your spirit a lift that you then take into your interactions with everyone else you meet. With just a few simple words to one person, you can start a chain of positivity that extends from one person to the next and out to a whole bunch of others that you'll never even meet.

5. Smile!

Even in our non-verbal communications, we can make a difference. Nothing surpasses a wide open smile straight from your heart. Smiling at a stranger that you pass on your morning walk or in the supermarket will not only lift your own spirits but also those who are fortunate enough to be graced by your sunshine.

It takes a concerted effort to brighten someone's day but, over time, it becomes natural and organic. You actually have the power to shift and change the world simply by treating others with love, compassion and understanding.

Most importantly, how you treat everyone and everything in your life is essentially a reflection of how you are treating yourself. When we start focussing on how we can inspire others to find their inner beauty, we are actually connecting in the most elemental way to our own authentic self.

in the company of strangers

I remember going to a weekend personal development course some time ago and being absolutely petrified that everyone else would know more than me and that I would sound like an idiot if I opened my mouth.

Then, during a guided meditation, the facilitator said to the group: "Remember that everyone is just as scared as you as you are of them."

Bang! Wow! I nearly jumped out of my seat! I'd been so caught up in worrying that I wouldn't be as good as the next person when, all this time, it seems that they were worrying that they wouldn't be as good as me … or the person on the other side of them … or the one in front.

From that moment onwards, I've had the courage and confidence to speak my mind and be totally comfortable in the company of strangers. We are all part and parcel of the same universal energy force. We all have our insecurities and fears and challenges.

There's no-one better than me and I'm not better than anyone else.

Okay – so now we've got those fears and insecurities out of the way, let's look at how we can 'blossom' into the wider community.

Researchers have found that we are more satisfied and fulfilled when we contribute in some way to our community. Patanjali picked it long before any studies were done, listing aparigraha – non-greed – as one of the yamas in his first limb of yoga: Don't be greedy with your skills and talents, he was saying; share your knowledge and gifts with those around you.

Helping others really is an instant pick-me-up – particularly at those times when you may be feeling down or lonely or in need of a change. You'll feel better about yourself, you'll expand your circle of friends and acquaintances, and your contribution will make a big difference in so many other people's lives.

You will recognise your own path when you come upon it because you will suddenly have all the energy and imagination you will ever need.
Jerry Gillies

So how can you help? We all have gifts and talents that we can share with others.

Perhaps you enjoy cooking … so why not bake an extra cake for a friend or neighbour.

Or you may have an awesome green thumb and only a small backyard. I'm sure there would be elderly people living nearby who could do with a hand in their yard or you could join (or start!) a local community garden.

Go online to find volunteering websites, social groups, community education programs and Council activities in your area. There's bound to be something that matches your interests and, if not, think about starting a group or class or program of your own.

The most important thing is to work within your passion as this will ensure sustainability. When you devote yourself to the betterment of others, it's easy to burn out as it often feels like an uphill battle with very little return. If you don't absolutely love what you're doing, you won't last long.

When you come upon a path that brings benefit and happiness to all, follow this course as the moon journeys through the stars.
Buddha

the magnificence of mother earth

Just as we nurture ourselves and the people around us, so too should we look after the very source of our existence: the beautiful planet we live on.

Patanjali's niyama, shaucha – purity – relates not just to our minds and bodies but to the world that surrounds us.

As a blossoming yogi, be mindful of how you tread upon the Earth. Ask yourself if there is anything more you can be doing to lessen your impact on the environment: Recycling your garbage; using food scraps to create compost for the garden; picking up litter that you might find on the streets?

Think, too, about nurturing your connectedness with nature. How often do you really stop and take a moment to soak in all the natural sweetness your senses are exposed to?

To walk along the beach and breathe in the crisp, salt, sea air.

To gaze in awe at a spectacular sunset.

To feel the raw growing energy of ancient trees in a rainforest.

To listen to the morning song of the birds outside your window.

When we take time to stop and smell the flowers in the universal garden, we can't help but feel part of something so much bigger than ourselves as we merge with the magnificence of Mother Earth.

breathe … bend … blossom

Let's be honest: A lot of people take up yoga to achieve a hot yoga body like the celebrities. The reason they keep coming back to class, however, is very, very different.

In my yoga studio, I have seen literally thousands of people transform before my eyes.

They become softer externally and stronger internally.

They make changes to how they eat and their bodies begin to beam with light.

Their eyes sparkle and their faces brighten.

They become more grounded – and yet their spirits soar.

They talk less but have more profound things to say.

They become fearless and more compassionate; confident yet humble.

Every time we twist and turn, bend and stretch, we are reshaping and molding ourselves – body, mind and spirit no longer the same.

I feel such a deep sense of gratitude to be a part of this deepening of spirit that so enriches their lives.

Because, with each magnificent blossoming yogi, I am inspired to continue along this path I have chosen.

In the same way, I encourage you all to be the light that shines around you – on yourself, on your families, on your friends, on your community and on the planet we call home. Just stay focussed, disciplined and carve out the destiny you desire as you blossom into all that you can be.

be confident

be courageous

be carefree

be compassionate

be creative

♥

*Be the change that you wish to see in the
world.*

Mahatma Gandhi

yoga definitions

terminology	literal translation	usage
abhyantara kumbhaka	within, internal (abhyantara); cessation of breath (kumbhaka	In pranayama, the cessation of breath (hold) after inhalation - when the lungs are full
agni	fire	Related to the thumb in mudras
ahimsa	non (a-); injury or harm (himsa)	Non-violence – the first yama in Patanjali's eight limbs of yoga
ajna	command or summoning	The third eye chakra, located between and just above the eyes
akash	ether	Related to the middle finger in mudras
anahata	un- (an-); beaten, hurt (ahata)	The heart chakra
anga	limb	In reference to Patanjali's eight (ashta) limbs (anga) of yoga
aparigraha	non (a-); greed (parigraha)	Non-greed – the fifth yama in Patanjali's eight limbs of yoga
asanas	seat or sitting down	Yoga postures or positions; the third limb of Patanjali's eight limbs of yoga
ashtanga	eight (ashta); limbs (anga)	In reference to the eight guiding principles of yoga defined by Patanjali
asteya	non (a-); stealing (steya)	Non-stealing – the third yama in Patanjali's eight limbs of yoga
aum or om	'It is' or 'will be'	Seed syllable said to be the sound of all creation and all living things; used as a mantra to aid meditation
bahya kumbhaka	exterior (bahya); cessation of breath (kumbhaka)	In pranayama, the cessation of breath (hold) after exhalation - when the lungs are empty

terminology	literal translation	usage
bandhas	lock or seal	A contraction of muscles to seal or lock energy into a specific chakra or chakras
brahmacharya	god (brahma-); to follow (charya)	Interpreted as sexual restraint - the fourth yama in Patanjali's eight limbs of yoga
chakras	wheel or turning	In eastern medicine, focal points in the body that receive and transmit energy
chin mudra	feather (chin); lock or seal (mudra)	Hand symbol used in yoga to direct energy
dharana	concentration or single focus	The sixth limb of Patanjali's eight limbs of yoga
dhyana	meditation	The seventh limb of Patanjali's eight limbs of yoga
dirgha pranayama	One of the pranayama breathing techniques	Long or prolonged (dirgha) breath (pranayama)
drishti	vision, sight, perception	A visual point used to achieve focus in yoga pose
guruji	darkness (gu-), destroyer of (ru-); title of respect (ji)	Respected teacher who dispels spiritual ignorance (darkness) with spiritual illumination
gyan mudra	knowledge (gyan); seal or symbol (mudra)	Hand symbol used in yoga to direct energy
hatha	sun (ha-); moon (tha) - signifying balance	A system of yoga introduced by Yogi Swatmarama in the 15th century to purify and physically prepare the body for meditation

terminology	literal translation	usage
ida nadi	lunar or left (ida); channel (nadi)	Energy channels associated with the left side of the body and masculine attributes
ishvara pranidhana	supreme being or divine (ishvara); surrender to or love for (pranidhanaI)	Surrender to the Divine - the fifth niyama in Patanjali's eight limbs of yoga
jal	water	Related to the little finger in mudras
jalandhara bandha	chin (jalandhara); lock or seal (bandha)	Chin lock or throat lock - a contraction of muscles to lock or seal energy into the throat chakra (visuddha)
maha bandha	great (maha); lock or seal (bandha)	Combining the three main locks – jalandhara bandha, mula bandha and uddiyana bandha
manipura	jewel (mani); city (pura)	City of jewels - chakra located in the solar plexus region
mudra	seal or symbol	Hand symbol used in yoga to direct energy
mula bandha	root or base (mula) lock or seal (bandha)	Root lock - a contraction of muscles to lock or seal energy into the root chakra (muladhara)
muladhara	root (mula); one's own abode (adhara)	Root centre - chakra located at the base of the spine
Nadi	tube or pipe	In eastern medicine, the channels through which energy is distributed around the body
Nadi shodhana	tube or pipe (nadi) purification (shodhana)	One of the pranayama breathing techniques
nasagrai drishti	nose tip (nasagrai); vision, focus (drishti)	Focal point (drishti) at or just beyond the tip of the nose

terminology	literal translation	usage
niyama	observance / restraint of the senses	The second limb of Patanjali's eight limbs of yoga
Patanjali		Often called the 'father of yoga'; author of The Yoga Sutra of Patanjali which incorporates the eight 'limbs' or guidelines for living a moral life
Pattabhi Jois		Founder of the Ashtanga Yoga Research Institute in India focussing on the vinyasa system of combining the breath with yoga movements
pingala nadi	solar or right (pingala); channel (nadi)	Energy channels associated with the right side of the body and feminine attributes
pranayama	lifeforce (prana); control (yama)	Control of the lifeforce through regulated breathing techniques; the fourth limb of Patanjali's eight limbs of yoga
pratyahara	away or against (prati-) food or anything taken into ourselves (ahara)	Withdrawal of the senses; the fifth limb of Patanjali's eight limbs of yoga
prithvi	earth; Mother Goddess	Related to the ring finger in mudras
puraka	inhalation	In pranayama, drawing air into the lungs
rechaka	exhalation	In pranayama, expelling air to empty the lungs
sahasrara	thousand-leafed lotus	Crown chakra located at the top of the head
samadhi	even (sama-) intellect (dhi)	The state of ecstasy; the eighth and final limb of Patanjali's eight limbs of yoga

terminology	literal translation	usage
santosa	peace; tranquillity; contentment	The second niyama in Patanjali's eight limbs of yoga
satya	truthfulness	The second yama in Patanjali's eight limbs of yoga
savasana	corpse (sava); pose (asana)	Corpse pose – used in relaxation
shaucha	purity; cleanliness	The first niyama in Patanjali's eight limbs of yoga
sheetali pranayama	cooling breath	A pranayama technique that lowers the body temperature by inhaling through the mouth while letting the breath flow in over the tongue.
sthira sukham asanam	stability (sthira); ease (sukham); seat (asanam)	"May my connection to the earth be steady and joyful"; "the yoga pose is firm but happy" - Patanjali
sukha pranayama	happiness, pleasure (suhka); breath (pranayama)	A pranayama technique that reduces stress
surya namaskar	sun, sun god (Surya); salutation, greeting (namaskar)	Sun salutation - A series of asanas traditionally dedicated to the sun god, Surya.
sushumna	spinal cord	The main energy channel passing through the spine from the solar plexus to the crown of the head
svadhisthana	self (sva-); dwelling isthan)	One's own abode; Sacral chakra - second chakra, positioned at the tailbone two finger-widths above the muladhara (root) chakra
svadhyaya	self (sva-); study, lesson (adhyaya)	Self-study; the fourth niyama in Patanjali's eight limbs of yoga

terminology	literal translation	usage
tadasana	mountain (tada) pose (asana)	Mountain pose
tapas	austerity	The third niyama in Patanjali's eight limbs of yoga
uddiyana bandha	flying up (uddiyana) lock (bandha)	Abdominal retraction lock
ujjiya	loud breathing	Audible breathing technique used during yoga practice; also called the ocean breath
vayu	air	Related to the index finger in mudras
vinyasa	in a special way (vi-); to place (nyasa)	A system of yoga connecting movement and breath
visuddha	purity; cleansing	Throat chakra
yama	to subdue, control (yam)	The first limb of Patanjali's eight limbs of yoga
yoga mudra	seal (mudra)	A seated posture to stretch the upper back and shoulders, also known as the Seal Posture
yoga nidra	sleep (nidra)	Sleep of the yogis, in which mind and body are at complete rest but with complete awareness